THE ELOQUENT LAY READER

*A Guide to Skillfully Preparing
and Delivering the Biblical Text
for Your Congregation*

Cindy Telisak

Good Shepherd
Publishing

Cover Design: Eyenegho D. John
Interior Design: Jen Henderson, Wild Words Formatting
Editor: Katie Chambers, Beacon Point Services LLC
Cover Photo: Stephen Radford on Unsplash

Published by Good Shepherd Publishing, Parker, Texas, USA

This book is available at discounts in bulk quantities for sales or promotional use. For general information on our other products or services or for technical support, please contact our Customer Care Department, at Good Shepherd Publishing, 4308 Church Lane, Parker, TX 75002. For more information about GSP products, visit our website at www.goodshepherdpublishing.com.

ISBN 978-0-9907808-2-3

Published in the United States of America

PRAISE FOR
THE ELOQUENT LAY READER

"With a passion to elevate the Word of God, Cindy provides a needed roadmap for all of us who seek to steward the reading of it in our collective worship. A most welcomed resource!"

**The Rev. Justin Lokey, Rector,
Faith Church, Anglican, Fairview, TX**

"Sermons help us understand and apply the words of the Bible but it is the reading of those words from the Holy Scriptures that present the perfect Word of God. *The Eloquent Lay Reader* is an essential manual for all who have the honor of reading the Scriptures in public worship in order to proclaim the Word of the Lord most effectively."

**The Rev. Don McLane, Rector,
Transformation Anglican Church, Rockwall TX**

"This comprehensive guide, written in an accessible and down-to-earth style, is a must for lay readers wanting to improve their skills, as well as for those responsible for lay reader training."

**The Rev. Deacon Carol Brooks,
Christ Church, Plano, TX**

"*The Eloquent Lay Reader* is full of incredible information, articulated well. I hope that lay readers (and even worship teams and choir members) will read it and take it to heart. It's so sad to see lay readers struggle with the Biblical text. Putting these ideas into practice will really connect them to God's word and deepen their Christian lives. Lay reader trainers should consider this as a standard textbook for their ministries."

The Rev. Deacon Jean Wolfe,
Anglican Church of Saint Paul, Owasso, OK

"This work is both useful and beautiful—readers will find the 'how to' instructions immediately useful to improve their reading; and beautiful, as Telisak invites readers into the joy, delight, and holiness of Scripture with her engaging style. I can't wait to get this work into the hands and lives of the readers of Scripture at the parish I serve!"

The Rev. Theron Walker, Rector,
Emmaus Anglican Church, Castle Rock, CO

TABLE OF CONTENTS

"Blessed is the one who reads
aloud the words of this prophecy,
and blessed are those who hear,
and who keep what is written
in it, for the time is near."

Revelation 1:3

SPECIAL NOTE FOR LAY READERS IN A HURRY

To be frank, I don't advise approaching this responsibility in a hurry. It's an honor and big responsibility to handle God's word in corporate worship. I want you to fully appreciate your value as a steward of this critical ministry. So please take a little time to go through all the first chapters and get a taste for what lay reading can be in your life—not only is your ministry a conduit for God's words for your congregation, but also a vital and nourishing part of your own formation as a follower of Christ. Let's not skimp on that.

But here's a pro tip: if you have a last-minute opportunity to read, or you need to brush up after some time away from the role, skip ahead to Chapter Six - Putting it all Together to see the process distilled and quickly accessible.

And don't miss the Bible book synopses in the Resource section for a quick context check for your particular readings. It will help, I promise.

INTRODUCTION

She stepped up to the lectern with her knees a little weak and a large frog creeping up the back of her throat. Pulling open the huge Bible to the marked page and staring at the first words of the passage, she saw "In the first book, O Theophilus—" *Oh no. What in the world is a Theophilus, and how on earth do you pronounce it? Well, just get through this, and hopefully, it will make sense if I go fast enough. Surely everyone here knows more than I do about the Bible! Which of my friends will be pulling me aside after church to razz me about stumbling over those crazy names? Will anyone even remember what the passage was about?*

Is this you? It has definitely been me. If you've ever found yourself in this situation, you know how uncomfortable it can be to stand in front of your congregation and show off your acute performance anxiety and your lack of biblical knowledge. You volunteered for this ministry because they assured you it was really easy. It's just reading, right? We can all read, can't we? We know enough about the Bible to bluff our way through, surely. But what difference will it really make in anyone's life anyway?

This book will give you so many ways to get the most out of your ministry of public reading that you'll get excited about it all over again. And so will your listeners!

I, too, have experienced that situation and have learned to conquer many challenges that might keep me from getting the most out of my ministry. I was a new lay reader once. I was a cocky little high schooler, raised in the church, and with a flair for the dramatic. When given the opportunity to read in church, I jumped at the chance to show off my mad skills. But the random Bible stories I had absorbed just by sitting in church all my life turned out to be insufficient to illuminate many unfamiliar passages.

I remember spending the duration of one particular reading trying to figure out, *on the fly*, exactly what the heck Paul was talking about in his six-line sentences with no pauses for a breath! I'm sure my congregation was thoroughly confused by the time I finished. Clearly, I should have prepared before I got up in front of people to wow them by my performance. Had I known then what I know now, the outcome would have been very different. (Thankfully, the Holy Spirit did his work in spite of my inexperience.)

In college, I studied theatre and communications, and even took coursework in general oral interpretation and oral interpretation of the Bible. I thought these would just be fluff courses; instead, the courses taught me skills that excited and encouraged me as the text sprang to life. I'll be forever grateful to my professor for codifying so much of the information that has helped me succeed as a lay reader. After graduation, I continued to hone my communication skills as a stage actor, a voice actor, a radio personality, and a teacher while also learning more and more about scripture. All these jobs have demanded a high level of preparation and helped me work toward my goal of winsome and persuasive communication, furthering my lay reader ministry.

This book is packed with what I have learned through those college classes and my experience as a lay minister. So I understand your plight; I have been there. I know all about the pounding heart, sweaty palms, dry mouth and the overwhelming fear of botching up the reading. I've asked myself at those moments, What was I thinking? Why do I keep signing up for this torture? The good news is that I found my way out to the other side. I learned that preparation produces confidence and calm.

I hope you've picked up this little volume because you serve your church as a lay reader or lector or some other similar job and want to bring your best to the task. If you volunteered and now find yourself a little overwhelmed by the job, I wrote this book for you. If you love the Bible and the people of your congregation, if your desire is to faithfully and confidently read the word of God aloud in your church to bring him glory, then you and I have the same goal, and this book is for you.

TWO OBJECTIVES

In this book, we'll focus on two main objectives: **understanding** the text and **delivering** the text. We'll outline ways to simply analyze a passage for basic understanding and we'll go over basic public speaking skills. That's the job in a nutshell. Conquer (or at least improve) these two areas and you'll be a successful lector or lay reader, and a blessing to your congregation as you share the life-giving scriptures. "But [Jesus] answered, 'It is written, "Man shall not live by bread alone, but by every word that comes from the mouth of God"'" (*Matthew 4:4*). As Christians, God's word is our very food. Come, be nourished, and feed others!

Of course you want to succeed and do a great job. Scripture is God's holy word, after all, and what better book could you read out loud to people who need to hear it? And as important as scripture reading is in the context of worship, there generally is a pretty low bar to entry into this kind of ministry. By that, I mean you don't have to go to seminary or probably even take classes. You just need to be willing. But that upside can also be a downside.

Without training and a little knowledge, you can feel a bit unqualified for the task. You don't want to embarrass yourself by reading poorly, stumbling over complicated words or sentences, or breaking out in a nasty sweat in front of everyone. Perhaps your knowledge of the Bible is a little sketchy. Perhaps you've never spoken in front of other people before. Or maybe you have just enough experience to realize you have lots of gaps in your understanding of how to get the most out of a Bible passage. Maybe you just need to figure out how to conquer stage fright, and you don't have a ton of extra time to go through a laborious system of text analysis and psyching yourself out of being a nervous wreck every time you're called on to read a passage in public. Perhaps you just wanted a way to serve your church and this seemed like an accessible way to do your part. Perhaps you've been a public Bible reader for a long time but want new ways to exercise your gifts. Or maybe lay reading feels a little stale and your reading has gotten a bit routine. This book can help you with all of that.

I have been there. But I have found lots of great ways to prepare so I feel up to the task I believe God has given me to do. Do I still feel a little nervous? Of course. But that adrenaline pounding through my veins is not a debilitating problem. It's a clue, a signal, that I'm about to do something important. In fact, I think of it as God-given super sauce to help me exercise this ministry in the very moments I need it most. And I am ready with God being my helper.

LITURGICAL WORSHIP IS UNIQUE

Even in this day of reported declining church membership across the US, our younger generations are finding themselves drawn to liturgical worship because of the high level of engagement and participation that differentiate us from the big box megachurch. Dr. Winfield Bevins, author of *Ever Ancient, Ever New: The Allure of Liturgy for a New Generation* writes, "For the past two years, I have

INTRODUCTION

traveled across the United States, Canada, and England visiting churches, cathedrals, universities, and seminaries. I have listened to dozens of young adults share how they have embraced Christian liturgy. I have heard stories about how liturgy is impacting many lives, and I have interviewed hundreds of young adults and leaders to hear their stories about how liturgy has impacted their faith. They are hipsters, authors, teachers, students, pastors, musicians, and people from all walks of life, but they have one thing in common: they have found a home in the liturgical practices of the historic church."

As lay readers, we play a critical part in the weekly liturgy, the grand retelling of God's story in corporate worship. The corporate worship service dramatizes the story of God's redemption of the world through Christ, throughout history. We join with Anglicans and other Christians all over the world who regularly recite the ancient prayers and perform the ancient practices that tie us to our spiritual forefathers and mothers through the ages. For many centuries, lay people were not allowed to assist as scripture readers; only clergy could do so. In the last few decades this has changed, and it's considered perfectly appropriate for trained (and sometimes licensed) lay people to bridge the gap between the people in the pews and the clergy who lead the service, preach the sermons, and celebrate the sacraments. We don't take our participation lightly, but serve at the altar with reverence and joy. Liturgical worship engages us in all our faculties—our minds, bodies, and spirits—as we stand, kneel, sing, eat, and drink at the Lord's table and hear God's word proclaimed. That's our part—the proclamation. On one hand, it might offer us great comfort to be in the glorious company of millions and millions of worshiping ministers all the way back to the temple of ancient Israel. On the other hand, when it comes time to read, we climb up to that lectern all by ourselves and the responsibility rests heavily on our shoulders.

Lay reading is a very important role in your church—you serve your listeners in the name of the Lord. It may not seem like you have the power to really affect the quality or tone of your worship service, but nothing could be further from the truth. Skilled readers make an impact on their listeners. Your ministry as a reader can positively affect the worship experience for the members of your congregation as a result of your skill, knowledge, and passion. By the way you read, you can change confusing Bible passages into spiritual epiphanies for congregants, as though they are hearing them for the first time. A comforting passage can penetrate deep into a hearer's life and help them connect to God in a way that is healing and restoring. In their life, your contribution is a huge blessing, if not a miracle. I'm guessing you have great passion, or else you wouldn't have signed up for a job that asks you to stand in front of a group of people—maybe a very large group of people— and put yourself out there, vulnerable and open to scrutiny. But you've done that, and I believe God will strengthen you for this critical task.

Skilled readers make an impact on their listeners.

Skilled readers paint vivid mental pictures with their voices, facial expressions, and the biblical text. Comforted by a reader's confidence, the audience relaxes and enters into the story and remembers the message long after the service, maybe even waking up to a life-changing spiritual truth conveyed in the reading. Your ministry as a lay reader can have a major impact in the spiritual growth of your church, in partnership with the Holy Spirit, and in combination with good preaching and teaching from the pulpit. What a fulfilling ministry!

As serious as it is to serve as a lay reader, please don't be overwhelmed or discouraged that the job is too difficult. It isn't. In this book, I'll present you with a toolbox full of useful tips and techniques to get the most out of your reading, not only for your audience but for your personal growth and formation as a Christian. When we stand up in front of the congregation, we can either dash it off unprepared and pray that we don't make a mess of it, or we can take a little time and systematically prepare. Then, even if our reading isn't perfect, we will convey a depth of knowledge that will enrich the hungry hearers and ourselves as well.

Many of us are uncomfortable with the idea of "performing" in church. That is completely understandable. I'm going to avoid the word "performance" as much as possible so that we don't begin to think that this ministry is about our own personal glorification. But in another sense, we are actually performing; we are *executing* a task in front of others. So as much as possible, I will use the word "execution" or "oratory" in place of "performance" or "performing" to make that important distinction.

Importance of Increasing Your Biblical Knowledge

If your biblical knowledge is patchy or hit-and-miss, you're not alone. Barna Research finds very little biblical literacy in the culture today. (87 percent of American households own a Bible—including atheists and skeptics. 50 percent of Americans engage with the Bible at least three–four times a year, and a third of adults say they wish they read the Bible more. We read in Barna's research "State of the Bible 2017: Top Findings" that the Christian Church is becoming less theologically literate: "*What used to be basic, universally-known truths about Christianity are now unknown mysteries to a large and growing share of Americans—especially young adults. For instance, Barna Group studies in 2010 showed that while most people regard Easter as a religious holiday, only a minority of adults associate Easter with the resurrection of Jesus Christ . . .*

The theological free-for-all that is encroaching in Protestant churches nationwide suggests the coming decade will be a time of unparalleled theological diversity and inconsistency.")

The Christian Church is becoming less theologically literate.

So even if *you* know your Bible, the chances are good that *your audience* may not. Bible stories that kids used to just pick up in the air are no longer common knowledge. We'll cover this in more depth later, but this is where you can help: by reading in such a way to convey the context and the important ideas and points. If you do this, the congregation's understanding of both the scriptural passage and the preacher's or pastor's related message increases. You are actually an agent for furthering the kingdom of God by clearly expressing his wonderful revelation to his people.

And you will be enriched, too, by the end of this little book. Reading and putting these ideas into practice will give you a huge dose of confidence, by showing you a simple step-by-step process for preparing yourself for this amazing task. Then it's just a matter of practice. The more you put these steps into action, the more second nature they'll become, and the process will pay off every time you step up to the lectern.

INTRODUCTION

---

*Growing in your personal love of scripture
and the richness of our liturgy are no
small incidental benefits to this process.*

You probably don't have the time to take seminary course work or study to be an actor. So I've boiled down years of training and experience into a succinct, manageable system to get you from cold reading to nuanced presentation in a short time. You'll get access to downloadable worksheets (www.goodshepherdpublishing.com/eloquentlayreader/resources) and lists that will streamline your preparation and enrich your time in scripture. With these tools you'll accomplish two objectives: **first**, to thoroughly prepare your text to maximize the experience for your listeners and **second**, to deepen your personal understanding of the biblical texts so that you'll grow as a disciple of Jesus and be able to knowledgeably express the texts. Growing in your personal love of scripture and the richness of our liturgy are no small incidental benefits to this process.

YOU NEED A SYSTEM

This book is organized as an all-in-one reference and guide to confident lay reading. To acquire the skills and background needed to communicate the great truths of scripture, you need to invest some time and employ a *simple process that is absolutely achievable*. No seminary degree is required. No membership to Toastmasters is needed. The skills needed to read the Bible aloud in the context of your worship service, or anywhere else, consist of following a simple checklist, praying, and practicing. *Confidence comes from preparation*, and my mission is to show you exactly how to prepare.

In the Resource section of this book, you'll see a very special tool: a synopsis of each book of the Bible, geared especially toward your needs as a reader. I've tried to point out particular background information that will help you frame your readings. For instance, it makes a big difference when reading Paul's encouragement to the early church in Philippi to know that he was writing from prison and that he did not expect to survive that incarceration. You can see how that affects the understanding and the interpretation of the very familiar passage, "Do not be anxious about anything, but in everything by prayer and supplication with thanksgiving let your requests be made known to God. And the peace of God, which surpasses all understanding, will guard your hearts and your minds in Christ Jesus" (*Philippians 4:6–7*). Context matters, and the last section of the book provides you with some very basic context to ground your readings. This resource is not exhaustive, and I definitely recommend combining it with more thorough commentaries, but it is a place to start, and a quick guide if you find yourself with a short time to prepare to read an unfamiliar passage.

I'm completely confident that you'll improve your public reading skills the very first time you put these principles into practice. I have trained many lay readers like you, and the results have been dramatic. These lay readers learned to slow down and look at the texts with analytical eyes, and they learned to intentionally improve their public speaking skills. In very short order, their readings took on new insight and excitement. They traded dread and fear for confidence and joyful anticipation at the next opportunity to serve. And members of their congregations took notice. They received comments like, "I always love it when you read. I get a lot more out of the readings." To have someone stop you after church and talk about how much they got out of the scriptures lets you know that you've made a difference. (Just don't let it go to your head!)

While the preparation skills in this book will help with any reading assignment, reading *the Bible* is quite different in my estimation. I believe *you* can expect to be changed because of your role as a lay reader. You'll be reading and digging into God's word, which is as true today as centuries ago when it was written. The Bible has the power to convict us, illuminate our sin, comfort us in our sorrow, and strengthen our faith. It is not a magic book with incantations or spells; it is not like a pharmacy of feel-good quotes or fortune cookie platitudes. Scripture is much bigger than that. The Old and New Testaments have a unified arc, telling the story of the history of mankind, our repeated failures at faithfully following God, and his amazing plan to bring us back to him. Now, that's a story! Do not be surprised if God uses this story of unfathomable love and grace to get your attention and change you from the inside out.

I encourage you to crack open this book right now and see for yourself how simple and logical this system is, how straightforward the checklists are, and how quickly you can implement them. You can be reading with passion and confidence by this Sunday! I pray this book opens up for you new levels of love for the Bible and new opportunities for you to share your passion with your congregation. Paul says in his epistle to the Romans, "So faith comes from hearing, and hearing through the word of Christ" (*Romans 10:17*). Your congregation needs you to vocally proclaim God's word with confidence and conviction!

The job of lay reader can be a deeply fulfilling ministry that allows you to impact the spiritual lives and growth of your congregation without ever stepping foot inside a seminary. Conversely, it can be an afterthought duty where you hastily read the words in front of you like you're reading the newspaper, completely missing the opportunity to grow, to serve, and to really be an enriching gift to your hearers. Which lay reader will you be? Flip open this book, and let's go! You can make a difference!

THE LITURGY AND YOU

Why Lay Readers are Important in Worship

The word "liturgy" comes from the combination of two Greek words: *litos* and *ergos* which combine to mean "the work of the people." This is our work as everyone present in a church service participates; God is the only spectator. The first Christians considered the public reading aloud of scripture along with the celebration of the Lord's Supper as the focal points of their gatherings. This "liturgical" worship continued the public proclamation of God's word that the Lord himself instituted for the Hebrew people. In the mid-sixteenth century during the Protestant Reformation, many of the churches that broke away from Catholicism changed their doctrines, but kept the same participatory style of worship, including scripture readings, Communion, similar prayers, creeds, and rich symbolism.

The Anglican Church, my spiritual home, sprang up as the English expression of the Protestant Reformation. Other denominations share the same reformed heritage and liturgical worship to some degree: Methodists, Presbyterians, Lutherans, Episcopalians, and others. The Reformation was a very tumultuous, complicated time of overturned authority systems, and a reclamation of some critical Christian doctrines that the reformers believed to have been lost or hijacked since the days of the early church. But the important takeaway for lay readers is the understanding that liturgical worship follows the basic structure for a weekly corporate gathering that has been handed down from first century Christian worship, which itself was informed by Jewish worship traditions from hundreds of years before. This ancient worship continues through the ages to offer a vibrant way of interacting with God in the company of fellow believers.

The convictions of the Reformers took hold of me as a teenager, giving me a strong belief that the scriptures of the Old and New Testaments are the ultimate authority for our lives, that salvation is not earned by works but only accepted as a gift of grace, that Christ's voluntary death on the cross and resurrection paid the price for my sin, that Jesus is exactly who he says he is, that each Christian has individual responsibility to answer the call of Christ and follow him alone, and that forgiveness is available for the asking. These reformed convictions guide my spiritual experience and understanding every day as I continue to grow as a disciple.

Through the past years of study, I've come to believe that the contents of the Bible are objectively true for solid, intellectually defensible reasons. At the same time, the Bible is full of mysteries that *can't* be explained by our understanding of science or empirical evidence—not now, and perhaps not ever. Yet, I believe, based on the integrity of the text, that the biblical narrative adds up to be the very best explanation there is for the reality we are living. I'm convinced that the good news of Jesus needs to be expressed and communicated as winsomely and competently as we humanly can, to bring more of God's beloved people into his kingdom.

HOW DOES THIS RELATE TO THE LAY READER?

In Anglican worship, the Bible is the foundation of our faith, and we are privileged to proclaim it boldly in our congregations. The first half of our weekly Communion service revolves around the oral recitation of several passages of scripture and then the preaching of a sermon by the priest, usually focusing on those scripture passages, The Ministry of the Word. (The second part of the Sunday service is called the Ministry of the Table, or Communion, which is a topic for another book.) Readings from the Bible are chosen for both personal and corporate worship in a systematic way through daily and weekly selections called the Lectionary. This rotating three-year list of passages assures that most of the entire Bible is read to the congregation, delivering a comprehensive and robust experience of the biblical text, not dependent on the preferences or whims of the clergy.

We Anglicans are also blessed with *The Book of Common Prayer* (BCP), largely crafted by Thomas Cranmer, Archbishop of Canterbury, in the early sixteenth century. Cranmer's inspired work lays out an orderly form of worship with prayers laden with scriptural passages and biblical phrasing as rich as boughs of grape vines burdened with ripe fruit. Our order of worship boldly exemplifies the centrality of scripture in the life of the Church and each individual Christian. This liturgical worship form is practiced by over 80 million Anglicans alone around the world to this day. This year, after years of scholarly and prayerful work, the Anglican Church in North America is releasing its own version of the BCP, which is an attempt to roll back some of the more recent innovations that had drawn it away from its original doctrinal moorings. This 2019 version intends to return Anglican worship to the foundational understandings of Cranmer and other pillars of reformed Anglican belief. The Church through the ages may shift off her foundations from time to time, but God is faithful to lead believers to return to the "faith once delivered to the saints" (*Jude 1:3*).

With the reading of scripture so central to the life of the Church since the beginning, and so critical for the lives of each individual Christian today, it follows that public scripture reading should be treated seriously and reverently. This is not the sports page we're pronouncing. This is living literature, God's word, preserved through the ages by God's design and by the blood of martyrs. Those of us who serve as lay readers owe it to the text, our audience, to ourselves, and to God himself to bring our best to the task. I believe you want to do exactly that, or you wouldn't be reading this right now.

WHAT EXACTLY IS YOUR JOB?

In addition to reading the weekly scriptures, lay readers may have other duties. They may have the privilege of assisting the clergy with distributing the elements, the bread and wine, in Communion. They may take consecrated elements to home-bound communicants. They may light candles, carry the processional cross, swing the thurible (incense burner), ring Sanctus bells, or other liturgical tasks. These are glorious duties that we share with people who have served at the altar through the ages, and they should be performed with joy and deep reverence. However, we won't cover those duties in this book. For help with those responsibilities, I happily refer you to your own clergy and diocesan or jurisdictional guidelines.

But in terms of your duties for the weekly readings, simply put, your job is to faithfully convey the plain meaning of the text—not to preach, not to intone, but to communicate what is happening in the text simply and effectively. This sounds easy enough, but as we'll see as we walk through the process, the experience is much richer than just engaging your vocal cords. Do you know how Olympic athletes make their sports seem so easy, so effortless? That apparent ease took years and years of grueling practice. Fortunately for us, the road to excellence isn't nearly that long or hard, but you will need to invest some focused attention. If reading scripture for your congregation is worth doing, it's worth doing well. You'll be making it look easy in no time! As Proverbs 22:29 reminds us, "Do you see a man skillful in his work? He will stand before kings; he will not stand before obscure men."

Your job is to faithfully convey
the plain meaning of the text.

It is a privilege to read God's word to the congregation, and we do need to give it the weight it deserves without simply laying on an unnecessary coat of seriousness. Many passages in scripture are really funny or have lots of sarcasm or irony. Other parts are sad and tragic, or glorious and exciting. Each passage needs to be read, understood, and conveyed so the audience gets an accurate and full understanding of what is going on. In this book, we'll learn to look at the text with an analytical eye and determine what each passage needs, in order to be read effectively. Come to the text humbly, willing to learn and be changed. Come with faithfulness, willing to devote the time to the process and eager to offer your skills and knowledge.

I highly recommend that you pray before studying your assigned reading and pray before orating your text. Ask the Lord to bring his words alive through you to the congregation. God had his words written for a reason, and he will help you convey that meaning to the congregation, the people he loves.

WHAT IS NOT YOUR JOB?

Let me take a little pressure off of you. There are several hard things about Bible reading for congregations that are *not* your job. For instance, you are not being asked to coax any deep hidden meanings out of the text. You are not being asked to preach or teach the congregation anything. That is your pastor's or priest's job. You are only responsible for expressing the plain meaning of the text (though you may begin to see new things as you go through our simple text analysis process). It is not your job to scold, lecture, entertain, or castigate your congregation. Let the text do that if that is the plain meaning. You are not the Holy Spirit, whose job it is to convict people of sin, comfort them in sorrow, or encourage them to rejoice and be glad. Let the Holy Spirit and the word of God do the heavy lifting here. A good general rule for life is to avoid using scripture to hammer people over the head (regardless of how badly you may feel they need it). You're the messenger, not the message. You read, and your pastor interprets that scripture to teach the flock.

Take comfort that your job is big enough to be richly satisfying, and leave the rest to the clergy.

And this one's very important: it is not your job to *feel* spiritual or holy or even completely up to the task. Our feelings hardly ever do our bidding or come when we call. How many times have you woken up on a Sunday morning and immediately the wheels came off your day? The spouse picked a fight, the kids squabbled among themselves, the coffee pot broke, and the last thing you wanted to do was to struggle through traffic for the opportunity to get up in front of a bunch of people and squeeze out a moving rendition of 1 Corinthians 13. We've all been there. We've all stepped up to read and felt like we were bringing nothing to the table. And we've been right. Even when we prepare, *and we should prepare*, nothing in our amazing arsenal of skills will convict our hearers' hearts of sin, or encourage the despondent, or mobilize the lethargic. Only the Holy Spirit can do that. So, put yourself, your skills, and your emptiness in God's hands and offer him what you have. It will be enough because *he is everything*. To lift a quote from St. Paul, "But we have this treasure in *jars of clay*, to show that the surpassing power belongs to God and not to us" *(2 Corinthians 4:7)*.

I heard a story not long ago about a young man with Down's syndrome who got up to read a passage in front of his congregation. Everyone braced themselves for a long, painfully halting, stumbling rendition. The tension and concern were palpable in the room. But that young man understood the text and read it with passion and humility. He wasn't trying to preach. He wasn't trying to look good. He wanted to communicate the simple but profound truth of God's word. His hearers were reduced to tears, as the power of God was exemplified both in the words themselves and in the vessel God had used to express them.

Humility is the key. Consider yourself no better and no worse than what God says you are, with the full understanding that you are just giving back to him what he first gave you.

SPECIAL NOTE FOR WOMEN READERS

The Bible authors were all men. For God's good reasons, all the Bible writers were men placed in strategic times and locations to transmit his words to us through the ages. Though many women are talked *about* in scripture, no women authored any books of the Bible. For us as female lay readers, does this change anything about how we read? I don't believe it should. We still put ourselves in each writer's shoes and read as we believe that author would have said those words for the first time. Again, *the readings are not about us, whether or not we are male or female.* They are about God, and we all, women and men alike, have a universal need for the stories and admonitions and encouragements in his word. Women are just as capable of transmitting those stories and admonitions as are our brother believers.

SCRIPTURE AS LIVING LITERATURE

The Global, Ancient, and Immutable Value of the Bible

Justin Peters, noted pastor and apologist, has said, "If you want to hear God speak, read your Bible. If you want to hear God speak audibly, read your Bible out loud."

To do our job fully, we need to have a good understanding of the Bible's text, stories, characters, history, and purpose.

REVERENCE, BUT NOT IDOLATRY

With a text that is both laden with gravity and ignored in its ubiquity, we can fall prey to two opposite problems: we can treat it with either blind veneration or with over-casual familiarity. Are the Bibles in your house displayed but not read? Dusted infrequently and cracked open only on special occasions? Used to record genealogical information but not much else? Or is the problem that they are all over the place, used as drink coasters, read in fits and starts, but not taken seriously? Do you have scripture references on your T-shirts but don't really know their context? It's time to take a closer look at this incredible collection of writings and get a rounder, fuller understanding of exactly what lies between the creaky, leather-bound covers. The last section of this book will give you a quick reference to basic context points for each book of the Bible. But right now, let's take a look at some very interesting facts about this amazing ancient text.

WHAT THE BIBLE SAYS ABOUT THE BIBLE

Whatever our culture thinks about the Bible now, it's clear that the men who wrote it, and the audiences they wrote it for, believed God's word was powerful and unmatched in our human experience. The Bible itself has a lot to say about the words God speaks and their efficacy. Through both the Old and New Testaments, God's word is lauded above all other communication we can ever experience. A few examples:

Isaiah 40:8   "The grass withers, the flower fades, but the word of our God will stand forever."

1 Timothy 4:13   "Until I come, devote yourself to the public reading of Scripture, to exhortation, to teaching."

2 Timothy 3:16   "All Scripture is breathed out by God and profitable for teaching, for reproof, for correction, and for training in righteousness…"

Hebrews 4:12   "For the word of God is living and active, sharper than any two-edged sword, piercing to the division of soul and of spirit, of joints and of marrow, and discerning the thoughts and intentions of the heart."

Romans 10:17   "So faith comes from hearing, and hearing through the word of Christ."

WHAT EXACTLY IS THE BIBLE?

Simply put, the Bible is a single collection in two "testaments" or covenants, of books written between about 1400 BC and 95 AD. These books were written by more than forty men inspired by the Holy Spirit to record the history of the universe, starting with the creation in Genesis and concluding with the prophecy of the end of the world and the coming of the kingdom of God in Revelation. The books of the Bible trace the story of God creating humans and giving them the perfect life in the Garden, the fall of all people into sin and a broken relationship with God, and then God's long-game to redeem humanity through Jesus Christ and to restore the relationship between himself and his people. This history of humanity includes graphic examples of every kind of human inclination—jealousy, fear, lust, oppression, betrayal, anger, trust, faithfulness, victorious faith, gentleness, forgiveness, and more. We see ourselves in all our human weakness on every page. But most importantly, we see God's steadfastness—his unchanging goodness and love—and the promise of ultimate victory.

An elite class of scholars called scribes first painstakingly copied the books of the Bible. These men devoted their lives to the scrupulous task of accurately copying the scrolls of the scripture so God's word could be disseminated to the people over large geographic areas. In this way, even as scrolls gave way to clay tablets, animal skins, and then paper, enough copies were made that even with slight variations and imperfections, we have a solidly reliable understanding of what the original authors wrote. Monks took over the job of making copies of the Bible until Mr. Johannes Gutenberg was kind enough to invent the printing press and relieve a lot of poor friars from terminal carpal tunnel syndrome. I recommend *A Visual Theology Guide to the Bible: Seeing and Knowing God's Word* by Tim Challies and Josh Byers for a fascinating look at this process of scriptural transmission. There is not room here to go into a lot of detail about the science of textual criticism, the scholarly pursuit which examines the ancient manuscripts to determine authenticity, but I happily refer you to Josh and Sean McDowell's authoritative work, *Evidence that Demands a Verdict,* as a great place to start. It's fascinating to trace the transmission of these texts from centuries past to the present day.

Here are a few interesting facts to support the notion that the Bible should be taken seriously:

- The Bible is easily acknowledged as the most influential book ever written.

- It has been estimated that five–six billion copies of the Bible have been printed since 1815.

- People have fought and died to see that it was faithfully transmitted, preserved, and made available to people all over the globe.

- People have died gruesome deaths for standing firm for the message it conveys—the radical message of God's redemption of the world through Jesus Christ.

- The Bible has been smuggled into hostile places as a liberating agent; it has brought literacy and a better standard of living to whole nations.

- Because of the immense power of its words, people have used it as a weapon for good and have also twisted it as a weapon of evil.

- But since we believe it is indeed God's word, we know that it will ultimately reflect God's perfect will.

- Rumor has it that the Bible is the most shoplifted book in the world, though solid evidence is hard to come by.

- The Bible wasn't broken up into chapters and verses until at least the 1200s, and our current system wasn't created until 1551 with the work of Robert Estienne. The headings over sections of scripture found in some translations are also new additions and not a part of the original text.

- When we read the Bible out loud to our congregations, we are bringing this singularly world-transforming message to life.

- Nowadays, Bible apps on our phones can read the Bible to us!

GOD'S SELF REVELATION

We serve a God who wants us to know him. He has revealed himself over thousands of years through the Bible authors, who weren't making up stories but were either chronicling their history as it happened or relating stories told faithfully over generations for the benefit of later generations. From these folks' amazing encounters with God, we learn about his character. We learn that he is omnipotent, omnipresent, omniscient, and any other "omni" we can come up with. Through his laws and covenants, we learn what is important to God. All through the scripture, God explains his ultimate plan for reconciling us to him, though we often reject it and are just as blind to it. He shows us how he designed us to live with each other and how to form a healthy community, warning us against harmful behavior while also displaying both his love and justice. In the same way we study the art of a painter to learn about him, so God's word and his creation teach us about him. In the scripture, Jesus tells us that he is God—that he is the great "I AM," the good shepherd, the vine, the door, the way, truth, and life. Just about everything we know about Jesus, we learn in scripture.

NOT MAGIC

And though the words of the Bible are divinely inspired, they are not magic—we do not quote scriptures as incantations. Some people treat Bible verses like stand-alone platitudes, removing them from their contexts and slapping them on coffee mugs to casually inject God into the start of their day. Others treat the Bible like a Ouija board, cracking open the pages at some random spot and poking their fingers down on the page, expecting a special revelation or direct message from God. These are gross abuses of the Bible and lead to nothing but misery. Jen Wilkin in her book *Women of the Word: How to Study the Bible with Both Our Hearts and Our Minds* calls this the "Magic 8 Ball Approach." She says, "The Bible is not magical and it does not serve our whims, nor is its primary function to answer our questions. The Magic 8 Ball Approach misconstrues the ministry of the Holy Spirit through the word, demanding that the Bible tell us *what to do* rather than *who to be*. And it's dangerously close to soothsaying, which people used to get stoned for. So, please. No Magic 8 Ball."

If we take the Bible at face value, respecting each genre of biblical literature and not twisting the intent of each of its authors, we will find the Bible to be a bottomless well of wisdom with this astonishing message: *God made us to worship him, and in spite of our refusal to love and obey him fully in return, he sent his only Son to pay the debt and bring us back to him.*

THE BIBLE FOR THE WHOLE WORLD

The Holy Spirit-inspired writers spoke Hebrew, Greek, and Aramaic, and then through the ages, the words have been translated into hundreds of languages. We have a direct mandate from Jesus that eventually all nations must hear about God and his plan for humanity (Matthew 28:19, "Go therefore and make disciples of *all nations*, baptizing them in the name of the Father and of the Son and of the Holy Spirit . . . "). According to Wycliffe Bible Translators, the world's foremost scripture translators, as of October 2018 at least some of the Bible has been translated into 3,350 languages, the complete New Testament has been translated into 1,534 languages, and 683 languages have the entire Bible. This sounds like a lot, but estimates are that two billion people still do not have Bibles in their own language. Many who understood the saving power of God's word dedicated their life's work to translating the Bible. They are the most important words ever committed to writing and hearing. We will do well to not take for granted our free and open access to scripture, or our dozens and dozens of available English translations and Bible commentaries.

BIBLICAL LITERACY, OR THE LACK THEREOF

As we've mentioned, even with all those Bibles, people aren't reading them for themselves. The youngest generations among us are the most biblically illiterate generation since the 1950s. We used to be able to count on cultural awareness of general biblical principles or Bible stories, but not anymore. A casual conversational reference to Noah and the flood or David and Goliath may get you blank stares. Therefore, we cannot assume our hearers are familiar with the passages. This makes our job that much more important. We can't read these stories in church thinking "Everybody knows this one. I can just whip through it." Instead, we must always come to the text assuming that our hearers are experiencing the story or the passage for the very first time. Even if they've heard it a hundred times, perhaps *this time*, with your expressive rendering, they will hear it deeply for the very first time.

STUDYING FOR PUBLIC READING VERSUS STUDYING FOR DEVOTION

As lay readers, we have to commit to knowing our text. Yes, it's a really big book, but aside from a few translation differences, it never changes. It has remained essentially unchanged for centuries. We can, over time and with persistence, come to know what's in it. We can come to have favorite parts. We can engage and wrestle with difficult parts. Together with great teachers and fellow students, we can dig and dig and dig and continue to mine rich resources for the rest of our lives from the biblical authors, who wrote at God's direction.

When studying the Bible, we can approach it in two chief ways, in order, one after the other. We first study what the passage meant to the writer and his hearers when the passage was written (a process called exegesis) and then we can work to figure out how to apply that meaning to our lives now (the process called hermeneutics). For our purposes as lay readers, we need to focus on exegesis as we prepare our readings. If we faithfully express the text's plain meaning as the original author intended, we will have done our job well. In the context of a church service, it's then the clergy's job to add any trickier bits of exegesis and add the hermeneutic piece in the sermon or homily. If we were studying a passage on our own or with a Bible study group, we would definitely be invited to dive into the hermeneutic, or life application, part of the learning. When preparing our passages to be read out loud, we don't need to worry about trying to convey what the congregation needs to do with the information. That's not our concern. We will go into exactly how to dig into the author's meaning of the text in the next section.

*For our purposes as lay readers,
exegesis is the area we need to focus
on as we prepare our readings.*

UNDERSTANDING THE TEXT

If You Don't Get It, Neither Will Your Listeners

GET TO KNOW YOUR BIBLE

The good news is that we don't have to attend seminary to be competent readers. We are not asked to preach on the text, just read it. But we cannot read it faithfully without a good foundation of understanding. Since the list of things to look for in a reading is not terribly long, you can commit it to memory over time. You'll get into good working habits when approaching the text that will serve you for a lifetime.

If you understand what you read, your audience has a much better chance of understanding it too, from the way you read. And that's really the whole point, isn't it? We want them to hear and understand and let God's word work in their hearts and minds. If you do not know what the reading is really about, especially if it contains extra-long sentences, complex concepts, or lots of unusual words or names, your audience may just be left shaking their heads when you're finished. Or worse yet, they may simply let their minds wander to more interesting things, like the announcements in the bulletin or what's in store for lunch. Rivet your listeners with God's word and they will receive most, if not all, the message they came to church for.

KNOW THE CONTEXT

You've probably heard that the most important three words in real estate are "location, location, and location." In carefully interpreting scripture orally, the most important three words are context, context, and context. Anchoring your understanding of the passage in its proper context is as important as skillfully delivering the passage. Christianity is not a religion of tales and fables, but is grounded in fact and history. Thus, to make sense of the Bible, we must consider the work as a whole. The entire canon has a timeline and a literary arc, from Genesis to Revelation. Each book has a purpose in supporting that arc, with its own content and literary style. Many have chopped up the Bible into little bits and touted it as a collection of proverbs or truisms, like a sack of fortune cookies or an anthology of self-help affirmations. Some do it out of ignorance; others, for more nefarious reasons. But either way, this damages the general understanding of God's word. All 31,102 verses of the combined Old and New Testaments have roles to play, but only as a part of their greater context. Author Greg Koukl teaches and lives by the axiom, "Never read a Bible verse," meaning that all scripture verses need to be read and understood by carefully considering their neighboring verses and even similar passages in different parts of the Bible. The Bible interprets the Bible. The only way you can "make the Bible say anything you want," as some have accused, is to rip passages out of context and assign them an alien interpretation.

In carefully interpreting scripture orally, the most important three words are context, context, and context.

UNDERSTANDING THE TEXT

Here's a good example found on coffee mugs and bumper stickers everywhere: Philippians 4:13 says, "I can do all things through him who strengthens me." Lots of folks take this isolated verse to mean, "I am an unstoppable force with God as my wing man." But if we zoom out a bit and read the entire short chapter, we see a completely different point. Paul is talking to the church in Philippi about his faith in God's provision and thanking them for providing financial resources to him. He talks about how he has suffered shipwrecks, beatings, and being left for dead, but despite these horrible hardships, Paul is content in any circumstance: "I know how to be brought low, and I know how to abound. In any and every circumstance, I have learned the secret of facing plenty and hunger, abundance and need. *I can do all things through him who strengthens me.*" So rather than a twenty-first century self-affirmation, this is an expression of total trust and contentment in God, regardless of the bank balance or even the state of physical health.

This could put a very different spin on the vocal interpretation.

To paraphrase Gordon Fee and Douglas Stuart in *How to Read the Bible for All Its Worth*, "A Bible passage can never mean what it never meant." Meaning, if it didn't mean a thing in the first century, it can't mean it now. We are not at liberty to take a short passage out of context and put a new or novel interpretation on it to suit our current purposes.

If you have the opportunity to read a passage of scripture you've chosen yourself in front of an audience, make sure to choose a long enough passage to complete a thought. If you are assigned to read a particular passage, especially an incomplete passage, you, as the reader, should help fill in the listeners' gaps of understanding by the way you read. In other words, either provide enough context, or help the hearers infer the context by the way you read.

When *you* understand what you're reading, your audience will understand the point, and that may be the first time the point has *ever* been made clear to them. And that goes in the win column.

BREAKING IT DOWN

So to get that understanding, where do we start? We start with reading the passage in our heads several times to get the flow of the words. Then we can begin asking some critical questions:

- Who is the writer? The Bible was written by more than forty men, each with his own context, motivation, style, and audience.

- When was it written and under what circumstances?

- Who was his audience?

- What occurrence prompted him to write, inspired by the Holy Spirit?

- Do you understand what you're reading? Does the plain meaning make sense to you?

- Can you restate the overall point of the reading?

- What is the most important point?

- Can you see the logic of the story or argument and use the supporting text to get from one important bit to another?

Turn to the reference section for a summary of each book of the Bible and significant information and themes they contain. If you're interested in further information, good study Bibles have extensive information at the beginning of each book that you'll find really helpful. Footnotes at the bottom of each page shed light on particular verses that may seem a bit enigmatic. Good scripture help is never far away.

Note: We briefly touched on this before, but it bears repeating as we begin to analyze the text: some Bible translations have added section headings throughout the chapters. For instance, above the text of Mark 1:1 in the English Standard Version (ESV) we see the heading, "John the Baptist Prepares the Way." Keep in mind that those section headings were added by the translators and do not appear in the actual text, and may or may not add to your understanding of the passage. At my parish, we consider it best practice to omit reading those added section headings. They were not intended as artificial breaks by the books' authors. Do your best to ignore them. If your passage begins at the first verse of a chapter, it doesn't hurt a thing to go back a chapter and see if the text naturally flows from one "chapter" into the other without a break.

And a special note for the Psalms: Sometimes you'll see the word "selah" in the text. There is some speculation that this word was a musical notation, as many of the Psalms were meant to be sung. As a result, we don't usually read that word "selah" when we come upon it. Just like we wouldn't read the words "go back to the chorus" if we were reading song lyrics out loud.

KNOW YOUR GENRES

What is the genre? We'll spend time on each book of the Bible in the reference section, including the distinctiveness of the genres, but in general, here are some things to note about each type, or genre, of Bible book:

HISTORY: The historic books generally tell stories of the Hebrew people, with a series of events, places, and people. These books tell the stories of scores of generations of people living their lives as God's plan moved forward, beginning with Genesis.

PROPHECY: Prophetic books relate God's word delivered to anointed prophets at different points of Israel's history. Sometimes the prophet's pronouncements came to pass immediately; others in Israel's near future, and still others are yet to be realized.

POETRY: Several biblical writers utilize poetry and song, with symbolism, artistic language, rhythm, and artistic craft (e.g., the Song of Moses, which is a passage from Exodus; the Song of Solomon; and the Psalms).

WISDOM: The books of Job, Proverbs, and Ecclesiastes fall into the wisdom category. Proverbs especially is the compilation of wise sayings of King Solomon, who asked for and received special wisdom from God.

GOSPEL: The Gospels, Matthew, Mark, Luke, and John, are direct or reported eyewitness accounts of the life of Jesus that include historical content, parables, stories of healing, sermons, and prophecies.

EPISTLES: Some scholars distinguish between "letters," which are personal and usually addressed to one person, and "epistles," which are usually directed at a church or group of churches in a region. For our purposes, we will group them together, because the point for us as readers is that we are speaking as the writer to a single recipient or group of recipients who have a unique problem or concern which the author addresses.

APOCALYPTIC: The Book of the Revelation of John is the only book in this category. Revelation describes the Apostle John's vision of the end times. This book is full of symbolism, fulfilled prophecy, cataclysmic battles, and the ultimate fulfillment of God's plan for his creation with Jesus on the throne. Though apocalyptic *passages* also occur in the book of Daniel and some of the prophets, the Revelation of John is definitely in a category all its own.

Why is genre important? As a reader, you can be much more informed if you understand how the style of writing informs the words themselves. Instead of getting wrapped up in the complicated symbolism of Revelation, for instance, you can focus on the fact that John was reporting fantastic visions that even he clearly didn't understand. In the poetic Song of Solomon, especially popular at weddings, the joy is to put yourself in the middle of the beautiful love story, unabashedly paralleling the relationship between Christ and his Church. The language is fairly explicit—a bit challenging for us to read in worship! In historical books, we may find ourselves reading accounts of battles and massacres, of sinful abuse and tragedy. The Bible does not flinch from reflecting a raw, graphic portrait of fallen humanity throughout history. As readers, we need to be ready to grapple with that kind of text and relate it honestly to our listeners.

READING THE TEXT FOR MEANING

Here's the fun part of getting ready to read, in my opinion. As you prepare to read, you will mine the jewels of meaning out of what might otherwise be a dull recitation of either an obscure or overly familiar passage. In just a few steps, you'll take an old passage you thought you knew and bring it much more to life. Maybe you'll take a passage that's brand new to you and see for the first time how it fits into the overarching narrative of the Bible, or how it applies to your own life. Let's look at the steps in order.

1. Read the text. Read the passage in several translations or paraphrases to get a fuller picture of what's going on. Different translators use slightly different words to express thoughts and

ideas from the original languages. Combining these ideas can fill out your understanding of the passage. If you use an online resource like Biblegateway.com this exercise is really easy as you can just bring up the passage and toggle through several of your favorite versions.

2. Read it again and look for details you missed the first time.

3. Back up several paragraphs to see what came before your passage. Lectionary readings are cut up into particular pieces—usually for good reasons, though sometimes they may leave out important context points.

4. Begin thinking about why the writer chose to relate this story or express this thought to his audience. Was he telling some history? Answering a question? Addressing some need? Combating false teachings or practices? For example, Paul's letter to the church in Galatia intended to set them straight regarding some false teaching that had infiltrated the church. He goes over some critical doctrines that had come under attack and scolds the Galatians for allowing themselves to be drawn off track. This book then not only straightens out the first century church in Galatia but points up some key beliefs we need to take to heart here in our own time.

5. Briefly jot down the main ideas or events of the reading in your own words. If you can summarize the main points or flow of the passage, you'll be able to relate it to the congregation so they also will really get what is going on.

6. If you get stuck on a passage that just doesn't make sense to you, check the footnotes in a study Bible, or a good Bible commentary for help. Commentaries are available for free online or in printed volumes by hundreds of different authors. They are available as complete Bible commentaries or as volumes covering a single book of the Bible. The choice of

commentary is highly personal, so get recommendations and shop around for one that is helpful to you.

7. If the passage meaning is still perplexing, call in a lifeline and phone a friend. Text your pastor or priest, or call someone who you think has a pretty good working knowledge of the Bible and ask them to shed some light for you.

CREATING YOUR VISUAL ROADMAP

A Careful Plan Gets You From
Point *A* to Point *B* in One Piece

Now that you understand the finer points of the passage, let's look at how to mark up your text and create a visual roadmap for vocally bringing out the critical elements.

MARKING THE TEXT

1. Type out your own copy of the text. Alternatively, you can cut and paste the text out of an online version, say, from Biblegateway.com (You can choose from hundreds of translations and paraphrases on that site. Pick the one your church prefers.) But typing it out will help you slow down and see every word of the passage without skimming over thoughts too quickly. So if you're willing, typing it out is better than cutting and pasting. Format the passage in a large font and make it double-spaced because you're going to need room to write and mark up your page.

2. On your typed page, begin marking your text. Use pen, pencil, markers, crayons, or whatever you like best. Use colors that alert you to important words or emotions. I encourage you to come up with your own system, but I'll share my marks with you as a place to start. I sometimes try to match colors with emotions, like red for anger or fear, blue for peace and calm, and green for action or important concepts, though I'm not a slave to a color chart. I use forward slashes to help me remember to pause. A double slash tells me to take a big pause for a change in tone or a lapse of time or change of scene. As you design your own system, get just creative enough to be useful—you can underline, highlight, or circle. You can bold words while you're still typing. Practice a bit and you'll learn what works best for you. (See page 71 for an actual example of marked text.)

- **Comparisons and contrasts:** One example is found in Psalm 68:2–3 "As wax melts before fire, **so the wicked shall perish** before God! **But the righteous shall be glad**; they shall exult before God . . . " Many passages, either single verses or paragraphs, compare and contrast the wicked and the righteous, just and unjust, life and death, regenerate and unregenerate, and many more. If you miss a contrast, you can miss the point of the passage.

- **Lists:** Pay attention to each item in a list, such as the one found in Galatians 5:22, "But the fruit of the Spirit is love, joy, peace, patience, kindness, goodness, faithfulness, gentleness, self-control; against such things there is no law." Lists require the reader to use careful pacing. It's easy to rush through a list and not give each item its due. I will sometimes add a slash between each list item to slow me down and remind me to give each one ample expression.

- **Connecting words, like "but," "therefore," and "so":** These special words alert us to how biblical concepts work together or build on one another. The old saying goes, "When you see a 'therefore,' go back to see what the 'therefore' is there for." The "therefore" section of the text is about to answer a "why" question that came previously in the text. Help the listeners understand this. Here's Romans 5:1: "**Therefore**, since we have been justified by faith, we have peace with God through our Lord Jesus Christ." (This is also one of those instances where we need to go back to the previous chapter to get the first part of Paul's argument.) Even if your reading can't answer the question to which the passage is the answer, your delivery will clue the listener in that something important came before. Maybe they'll go look it up, or hopefully, the preacher will fill in the blanks.

- **Repeated Words:** When a writer uses a word over and over in a passage, you can bet he means to emphasize that word or concept, and we need to help make that emphasis clear. My favorite example of this is the book of Ecclesiastes, where in six chapters, we find the word "vanity" thirty-two times. Do you think Solomon is trying to tell us something?

- **If / then construction:** This is an important and repeated argument construction we see in the Bible. Notably, God makes almost innumerable if/then pronouncements like this in Exodus 23, where he is promising Moses that an angel will lead them into the promised land: Exodus 23: 22, "But **if** you carefully obey his voice and do all that I say, **then** I will be an enemy to your enemies and an adversary to your adversaries." And Paul uses this to explain important concepts, like this in Galatians 2:21, "I do not nullify the grace of God, for **if** righteousness were through the law, **then** Christ died for no purpose."

- **Colorful words:** These are descriptive words that let us know about something extraordinary, either good or bad. These can be adjectives used to describe people, like ecstatic, delirious, angry, horrified, furious, terrified, zealous; or adjectives to describe events, like thundering, bloody, devastating, fiery (and thousands more). The narrative description of an amazing event can be very colorful, too, and a good reader will take advantage of those opportunities to fully express the extraordinariness of the situation. For instance, the story of Jael comes to mind, from Judges Chapter 4. Jael was a shrewd woman who lured the fleeing general of the Canaanites into her tent, pretending to hide him from the Israelites. She threw a rug over him to "hide" him, but then quietly took a tent peg and drove it into his temple, killing him, and securing the victory for the Israelites. You can't make this stuff up. What a great story to read with expression and gusto!

- **Pauses:** Pauses are powerful tools, and they must be used *very carefully*. Pauses are added by the reader to help the listeners mentally finish one part of a passage and prepare for the next part, or to denote the passage of time, or to strongly highlight particular words or phrases. Pauses say, "Heads up—this is important." Conversely, adding pauses where they don't logically belong can be terribly confusing for your listeners. You've signaled that they should take note of something, only to let them down. I see this happen a lot when the reader does not carry the momentum of a sentence to the end, but speaks in a jerky, halting way, which is very disconcerting to the listener. Figure out the point of the sentence, and don't stop or pause till you get there. Mark where you will pause ahead of time. As an example, let's pick on the Apostle Paul again. In his opening salutation in I Corinthians 1:4–8, he expresses a very complicated reason for giving thanks for them, "I give thanks to my God always for you because of the grace of God that was given you in Christ Jesus, **5** that in every way you were enriched in him in all speech and all knowledge—**6** even as the testimony about Christ was confirmed among you—**7** so that you are not lacking in any gift, as you wait for the revealing of our Lord

Jesus Christ, **8** who will sustain you to the end, guiltless in the day of our Lord Jesus Christ." Now that is one sentence, broken into four verses. If the reader isn't prepared for those twists and turns and doesn't carefully navigate those connected phrases and maintain the drive to the end, the listeners will get completely lost. Tiny pauses between the phrases help the hearers make sense of each one, but the congregation shouldn't be tricked into thinking the sentence is finished until it's actually finished. Again, single or double slashes can alert you to important places to pause in your reading.

Let's do a quick exercise. Beginning with our basic text analysis checklist, open your favorite Bible translation to Romans 2:12–29, or open it on your phone app/Bible website and

- Read it through.

- Read it again to find anything you may have missed the first time.

- Back up a few paragraphs before to get some context.

- Who is the author?

- To whom is he writing?

- Why did he choose to write this passage?

- In this passage, how many times does he use the word "law?"

- What two groups of people is he contrasting?

- How do these principles relate: law, obedience, circumcision?

- Can you state in your own words the major point Paul is making?

Do you understand the reading better after answering these questions? Great! Now that you understand the passage, mark your text in a way that visually helps you navigate the important words, concepts, pause points, etc. Can you read the passage aloud to yourself in a way that makes this point and these contrasts clearly?

Well done! That didn't take very long, did it? You're well on your way.

EFFECTIVELY
ORATING THE TEXT

Getting the Meaning of the Text
from the Lectern to the Back of the Room

---

*"What you say is the most important thing, but
how you say it could not be more important."*

—John Stott

In addition to the content of your reading, you have your personal context to consider: your environment, your own voice, your body which affects your voice, the acoustics, and the audience.

YOUR READING ENVIRONMENT

Is your reading environment a large auditorium, a small classroom, a vaulted cathedral, or an echoing gymnasium? Each of these structures will have a significant impact on your reading. Will you be amplified electronically with microphones and speakers, or are you going to use the acoustic amplification produced by your own voice? Are you speaking to a handful of people or a large group? How close are you to your audience? If you are speaking to people in an auditorium so large that it's hard to make out faces in the back row, you'll need to project and enunciate more and use larger facial expressions to communicate effectively than if you're reading for a group of people seated at a table right in front of you. The goal is to gauge your situation and adjust your execution appropriately.

We've all seen photos of actors in stage makeup who look a bit ridiculous and overdone up close. But that overdone makeup is what allows folks in the back row to see even the most nuanced facial expressions. By the same token, larger-than-life oral interpretation may be just what is needed when reading to a very large audience. Unless you have a good mic and great acoustics, plan on getting a good workout reading long passages to large groups. It can be physically taxing to simply read aloud because reading well uses a lot of your body and projecting well across vast spaces uses a lot of energy.

YOUR BODY IS YOUR TOOL

Just like a mechanic's wrench or a conductor's baton, you need your body to perform at its best to get the best results. We use a combination of many body parts in reading aloud: the legs, back, abdomen, diaphragm, lungs, throat, vocal cords, tongue, oral and nasal cavities, teeth, and lips. Seldom do we think about each of these individual parts while we read, but they all work together to produce the sound that people hear. Supporting all these individual parts is the body itself, specifically the posture of your body. A droopy or lopsided posture will negatively affect how all the individual internal parts work.

POSTURE

Good posture begins with standing up straight, with the weight evenly distributed on both feet. Both your hips and shoulders should be square and level. Your head should be up, at a comfortable angle—adjust the lectern or your printed text if you need to in order to see it well. You should consciously relax and keep your knees unlocked. If you stand with all your weight on one leg, with the other foot off to the side or behind or propped on the other, with your hips akimbo and shoulders slumped, you'll lose on at least two levels: you'll look unprofessional and disinterested, and your vital internal organs responsible for projecting your voice will not have the structural integrity they need to get the job done. Standing straight and squared to your audience will give you confidence and credibility and will allow your diaphragm, lungs, and voice to give you the support you need to communicate the text.

DIAPHRAGMATIC BREATHING

Reading begins with moving air through your vocal cords in order to make sound. We then shape that sound with our tongue, cheeks, teeth, and lips to form words. To convey meaning, we string words together and add facial and vocal expression. Something very simple and intuitive just got a lot more complicated! But take a deep breath. Once we take the process apart and carefully examine all the contributing pieces, we'll put it all back together again and I think you'll be amazed at the positive changes you'll see in your execution.

The diaphragm is a strong muscle in your abdomen that separates the bowel and lower organs from your lungs. This muscle contracts and relaxes to help you breathe. When it relaxes, it allows your lungs to expand and fill with air. When it tightens, this forces the air out of your lungs as you exhale to speak or sing. We breathe very naturally like this as babies and children, but as we get older, we begin to depend more on lifting our rib cages to fill and empty our lungs, letting our diaphragms get a bit lazy. Using our rib cages uses a lot more energy, is significantly less effective, and has very little strength of its own. Using this "chest breathing" forces the vocal cords to work overtime, risking painful straining. So people who rely on good breath control, like opera singers and yoga instructors, learn very quickly to focus on diaphragmatic breathing. We sometimes slip into chest breathing because of stress, which then is another critical reason to learn to willfully relax our body and use strong diaphragmatic breathing when we read out loud.

Like any muscle, the diaphragm can be exercised to help it gain strength and efficiency. This is where your vocal power will originate. The less amplification you have and the larger the group you're addressing, the stronger your diaphragm needs to be. You'll need it to project your voice long distances. If your diaphragm is not strong and you try to project your voice, you might be in danger of straining or losing your voice altogether.

THE VOCAL CORDS, MOUTH, SINUS CAVITIES

As the air is expelled from your lungs by your strong diaphragm, it moves up the trachea, or windpipe, and through your vocal cords. Then the air resonates inside your nasal and oral cavities; is shaped by your mouth, teeth and tongue; and then escapes as sound that we understand as words. To make the most pleasant sounding words, relax your body, stand strong, and ensure you are using all your vocalizing structures correctly.

So, ideally, when you read,

- you'll move to your position

- plant your feet

- relax your knees

- square your shoulders

- make eye contact with your audience

- take a deep breath down to your diaphragm

- refer to your text

- read in a strong voice appropriate to the size of your venue and your audience

REHEARSE OUT LOUD

Speaking out loud is significantly different than reading in one's head. This distinction cannot be overemphasized. You really will not have any idea how all your planning and preparation will look and sound until you actually execute it *out loud*. You never know what words or word combinations are going to trip you up until you enunciate them. Reading aloud is the time to test drive all the planning you did as you analyzed and marked your text. How does it sound? Do the pauses work well? Have you called out all the important colorful words? Will the contrasts and comparisons come across clearly to the hearer? Try recording yourself on your phone (video or just audio) to get a little reality check of how you look and sound.

If you're self-conscious reading the passage alone, how will you feel in front of an audience? One of the best ways to get over being nervous is to prepare thoroughly, by reading your passage over and over. Confidence comes from knowing what's coming and knowing that you are ready.

NO NEED FOR SPEED

The first thing most readers need to adjust with their reading is the speed. Often, they read much too quickly, causing the message to be lost. Nervousness or anxiety often results in reading too quickly, and we will address that painful challenge a little later. The fact is, people don't *hear and comprehend* as fast as they can speak. So keep your speed in line with what most people can follow comfortably. Also, vary your speed throughout your passage. Plan places in your reading that would be appropriate to slow down and emphasize particular words or phrases. Some parts work better if read more quickly and other parts work well more slowly. In fact, varying the speed of your delivery, as appropriate, will make your reading seem more natural and conversational. In normal conversation, we don't use a steady rate of speed all the time. A uniform speed and tone make us sound mechanical and unnatural. You are not Siri. You are not reading a phone book. (Ask an older person if you're too young to know what a phone book is.)

By the same token, reading *too slowly* can also be unnatural and distracting. Let's face it, listening to a too-slow reader can be painful. But worse than that, the meaning of the text will be completely lost and the opportunity wasted.

Some of the least effective readers have adopted a sonorous, sing-song delivery that doesn't resemble natural speech in any way. These are the folks we love to lampoon because this artificial style is in such regrettable juxtaposition with the glory of their text.

ADVENTURES IN PRONUNCIATION

Any casual stroll through a biblical genealogy will have even a seasoned lay reader stumbling and sweating. Those ancient names don't exactly flow off the tongue as they may have several hundred years ago. I always check my church's lay reader schedule to see who has drawn the Acts passage on Pentecost Sunday (Acts 2:1–11). This reading separates the seasoned from the rookie readers as they either read the list of cities and regions smoothly or they stumble and lurch.

To conquer this challenge, you can use several tricks: a) make up a reasonable pronunciation and stick with it, b) listen to an online Bible app narrator pronounce it and go with that, c) ask your pastor or priest, or d) mumble quickly and just get past it. Okay, maybe not the last one. But I'd say it is best practice to pronounce the name with sufficient authority that your listeners will never notice, and then be consistent. I'm serious. Don't get too worked up about these names. The most important thing is that instead of focusing on the list of names, you and your hearers can focus on the actual point of the text. If you are assigned an especially challenging passage, practice, practice, practice *until you can't get it wrong*. Then under the pressure of reading in front of people, your words won't fall apart on you.

But Bible passages also have words that can trip up readers even in our own language. Do you know the difference between *prophesy* and *prophecy*? Hint: one is a noun (a thing) and one is a verb (an action) and they are pronounced differently. Do you know what *propitiation* is, and how to say it? (See Romans 3:25 or Hebrews 2:17 in the ESV, for examples.)

Do you speak with an unusual accent? Does this affect your pronunciation in a way that will distract your audience? I have an old friend from the plains of West Texas who caused a subtle wave of chuckles through the congregation (among those of us who are easily amused) by reading how Adam and Eve realized they were "nekked." And the word occurs in that particular passage more than once. Needless to say, we weren't thinking nearly enough about the poor first couple who were about to find themselves out of the Garden without a paddle. We were snickering about "nekked." So, if your speaking style is a bit unusual for your environment (and you may need to get feedback from others to really get a handle on this), be prepared to make adjustments.

EXPRESS THE TEXT

Sometimes we feel like we're being insincere or showing off when we use a lot of expression in our reading. Though it is possible to overdo it, most folks err on the other end of the spectrum. Perhaps out of fear of drawing attention to themselves or perhaps with a laudable sense of reverence for the text, they underplay the text and sacrifice its richness. But the mismatch between the reader's demeanor and the text's drama, excitement, or violence actually disrespects the text and confuses the listener! Let me officially give you the permission you need to give animated expression to your reading and allow the listener to fully understand what's going on! People may sit up in their pews the first couple of times this happens, but that's because, sadly, they don't get to enjoy energetic readings with colorful storytelling very often. But trust me, you can impact the congregation in ways you may never fully appreciate, just by daring to honestly convey the text in front of you. Repeated practice and honest feedback from your pastor and peers will moderate this over time. But don't be afraid to push the envelope with your expression, until someone who you trust tells you to dial it back a bit. And then, don't dial it *all the way* back. When your earnest delivery inspires the congregation to sit up and pay attention, they, in turn, bring their a-game into worship, and your preacher may even step up his efforts as well!

Strike the right tone

You need to determine the most logical tone. This seems obvious, but sometimes as I listen to readers, they surprise me. So just to be clear, passages with funny or ironic parts should be read with the humor in mind, but serious passages should definitely convey a serious tone. Match your tone to the appropriate tone of the passage.

- **Humor:** Yes, there are some really funny parts in the Bible. In 1 Kings 18 the prophet Elijah taunts the prophets of the pagan god Baal when Baal fails to answer their cries for a miracle: "About noontime, Elijah began mocking them. 'You'll have to shout louder than that,' he scoffed, 'to catch the attention of your god! Perhaps he is talking to someone or is out sitting on the toilet, or maybe he is away on a trip, or is asleep and needs to be wakened!'" Good luck reading that in front of the congregation with a straight face! Or how about the story in John 9 of the formerly blind man being interrogated by the religious rulers about how he was healed. After recounting his story to them for the third time, he innocently *or sarcastically* retorts, "I have told you already, and you would not listen. Why do you want to hear it again? Do you also want to become his disciples?" Of course, this suggestion goes over badly.

- **Irony:** Some passages highlight the foolishness of people who ought to know better, but just like us, don't. We can chuckle because we recognize our own foibles even in the lives of Bible heroes. Think of the passage in Exodus 3 where God speaks to Moses out of the burning bush. Now, here is Moses, hearing the voice of God himself, out of a bush that is burning but never burns up, and God is telling him to go free the Hebrew people. How would we likely respond? Run away? Fall on our faces in fear? Swear to obey? Moses's response is to make excuse after lame excuse, to which God responds with no small measure of patience. The exchange between God and Moses would be hysterical if it wasn't really so serious.

- **Seriousness:** Many of the Bible's passages are sobering or tragic. These passages require careful and serious delivery. As one example, consider the passion narratives in the Gospels relating Jesus's trial, beating, crucifixion, and death. Nothing lighthearted about that.

- **Narrative:** Telling a story. This is always great fun because everyone loves a good story. Pretend you're reading to kids and use lots of animated expression. You may feel a bit self-conscious, but in reality, you are highlighting the text and letting it shine. (Think about the stories of Ruth or Ester or one of the Nativity accounts. The Bible is chock full of these captivating stories.) We think reading to kids is hard, but actually, keeping adults engaged can be much tougher. Don't be afraid to pull out the stops. I give you permission.

- **Dialogue:** Each character needs to have his or her own voice. When there is a conversation between people in the Bible, just like other types of storytelling, it really helps the listener if you can make a distinction between the characters with your voice. It doesn't have to be extreme, but help the listeners know which character is speaking. (Don't overthink sounding like God, just make that voice "heavier" than the character he's talking to.)

Means of expression

Expression is merely the ways you use your voice and your body to paint a picture of what is going on in your text. Think of the ways we read stories to kids to keep them engaged. We make faces, we do different voices, we vary our pitch up and down to create movement and tension as the story demands. We can use all of these same tools when reading scripture in a church service, albeit moderated a bit for our mostly adult audience.

Your face

Aside from your overall posture and body position, your facial expressions will have the largest impact on your reading. Your face is what people will notice first. Make eye contact to be sure you have people's attention, and then begin. Smile, if you're bringing good news from the Bible. Get stern if you're reading warnings from the prophets. This just makes sense. Your face needs to match the tenor of your words.

Your voice

Vocal inflection keeps the reading interesting and congruent with natural speech. When we discuss things we're passionate about, we have lots of vocal variability and power behind our voices. This tone insists that our listeners pay attention. And if you have a good understanding of the meaning and purpose of the text, your listeners will "get it." Success!

This is important: remember that people often put the most important words of their sentences at the end. They use the first part of the sentence to set up their point and then tie everything up as they conclude. So be sure to support your breath and your vocal intensity to the end of every sentence. Don't trail off in volume or drive before you get to the end. You'll leave your listeners puzzled and frustrated. See the sentence through!

Your hands

Hand gestures may also be appropriate and helpful to communicate meaning. If you're making comparisons, using your hands can help your listeners make clear distinctions. For example, "*on one hand* ABC, but *on the other hand*, XYZ." Or a contrast between near and far. When we look at the words of the text, these contrasts can seem self-evident, but when we are listening and so many words are coming at us at once, any traffic control is appreciated. Additionally, hand gestures help the listener imagine they are hearing the actual scripture writer address his audience. When we speak, and especially when we are conveying a message with urgency or import, we use our hands. This can instantly take you from "volunteer reader" to "almost the real thing." You've become an actor playing a role, allowing the listeners to imagine themselves seeing Paul debating the Greeks on Mars Hill, or Isaiah relating his vision of heaven, for instance. Now, this will mean that you need to know your text well enough that you can afford not to be tracing along the text with your finger, and that is another important goal in itself—knowing your text inside and out.

CAMERA READY

The more intrepid readers, especially in a training situation, may want to have themselves videotaped for critique later by the pastor, ministry leader, or peers. As scary as this might seem, many good things can be gleaned from this exercise. Not only will you see things that make you cringe, you will probably see even more traits that people respond to with great appreciation. It's important for us to know what we're doing well and what we need to improve. If you're ever called on to critique a friend, keep the positive elements in mind as well as the negative. Do unto others and all that.

SPEAKING OF NERVES

Let's just pull one of the biggest challenges out in the open and stare at it. Nerves. Anxiety. Heart-pounding, sweaty palms, dry mouth fear. How do we deal with this?

First of all, recognize that the adrenaline surge you get that makes your face flush and your mouth become dry is a God-given fight-or-flight response that is there to help you. You're not running from a mugger, but you *are* gearing up for a very important job. Don't try to suppress your body's response. Not only will you probably fail, but you can make things worse. Just go with it. Let your heart beat. Know that more blood is flowing to your vital organs and heightening your awareness. Breathe deeply and slowly. Don't hyperventilate. Thank God for giving you the ability to do the very important job he's asking you to do.

Second, be prepared. Even if you're terrified, your solid preparation will serve you well when you open your mouth to speak. You've studied, analyzed, prayed, and planned. You've practiced out loud over and over. Preparation gives confidence. You've got this.

Lastly, if the worst happens and you stumble a little (or even a lot), simply correct your mistake and move on. The great news is that *your listeners are on your side*. They want you to succeed! The very best news is that perfection isn't even the goal—faithfulness is. Grace covers us beautifully when we stumble and go on. As much as we want to do our very best in front of God and our friends, *we are not the focus*—God's word is, and God's word will survive a reading that we might feel was less than stellar. *Let it go* and do it again. And again. The more you read in front of people, the less you will struggle with nerves.

---

*The very best news is that perfection
isn't even the goal—faithfulness is.*

LOGISTICS

In some cases you may be able to read from your marked "worksheet." Even (or especially) if you read out of a large pulpit Bible, you may benefit from actually referencing a typed and marked page. When the time comes, simply slip your typed pages into the pulpit Bible or place them on the lectern and read directly from them. This allows you to read in front of people from the exact same notated text you rehearsed. The words will all sit in the same places on the page, with the same margins and markings. This system can eliminate unnecessary complexity by not changing the look of your text when you crack open the big Bible and everything looks different. With this method in mind, you should pre-place your printed text where you know it will be, well before the service or event begins.

However, some pastors or priests may have strong feelings about how the readings are done. If your pastor or priest prefers that you read directly from the lectern Bible, then you'll really need to memorize the way you have rehearsed the text so you can deliver it without your notes. You will want to practice beforehand with the actual Bible in front of you in order to make a smooth transition away from your marked worksheet.

If you just don't have the prep time to get your own text typed and marked, then it benefits you greatly to arrive early and make sure your reading, or readings, are carefully marked with ribbons or sticky notes or some other system. If someone else offers to mark the Bible for you, check their work—it's *you* up there in front of the people, not them, and you have a vested interest in not having any slipups.

Many lay readers keep their place on the page as they read by running an index finger down along the right or left margin of the text. This helps by allowing you to look away and make eye contact with the congregation from time to time without getting lost. If you have spent good quality time with the text in preparation, you should be quite familiar with the flow of the reading and that, too, will help to keep you on track.

In the Anglican tradition, the lay reader may begin and end with standard phrases to which the people respond. Before the reading, we can introduce the text with "Our first lesson is from the book of Genesis, Chapter 2 beginning at the first verse" (or a portion of that phrase). After the text we say, "The Word of the Lord," and the response from the people is, "Thanks be to God." Use the verbiage that your parish prefers. I find that in the heat of the moment, these phrases can sometimes slip my mind entirely—I recommend that you write them down and place them where you can easily find them before and after your readings, even if you think you'll remember them. The insurance of having them right in front of you is invaluable.

MICROPHONE SKILLS

Unless you're reading to a small group of people in a small room, you likely will be using a microphone. These come in all sorts of shapes and sizes, and they each require different treatment to get the best sound out of them. One of the most common setups is a unidirectional mic on a stand, either on the floor or on the podium or pulpit. With these mics, you need to have the business end of the mic pointing directly at your face, and you need to be as close to it as is physically feasible, sometimes a foot to six inches. It will be the sound technician's job to make sure you are amplified at a comfortable level for the people in the room. Remember to speak with a strong voice, breathing from your diaphragm for the best tone. If you must hold your own mic, keep your lips about one–two inches from the mic, point it directly at your mouth, and speak clearly.

Lavalier mics that clip to the collar of your clothing are fairly popular, and most come in a wireless style that allows you to wear it throughout the service without stopping to get hooked up just before you read. Also with the convenience of wireless technology, many churches have moved to using wireless mics with a flexible earpiece that wraps around your ear to hold it in place, connected to a cord and battery unit that slips into your pocket. These mics are space-saving, removing the need for a stand, and not too visually distracting for the congregation. Check that your mic is turned on, usually indicated by a green light, before the service begins. Point these mics at your chin, rather than your mouth, to avoid unwanted mouth noises. Then it's the sound tech's job to pull up your volume when it's your turn to speak. Also best practice: turn your mic *off* when you're finished to ensure that you are not accidentally miked for the whole congregation during a whispered conversation with the priest or during a last-minute trip to the restroom. Yes, it has happened.

Certain consonant sounds can push air into a microphone like a little explosion, with unpleasant results. "Fricatives" are the "f," and to a lesser extent, the "v" sound. "Plosives" are the "p" and "b" sounds. The plosive "p" is usually the hardest sound to moderate into a microphone. When too much air comes out in that quick instant, you'll hear the microphone complain and the tech will ask you to stop "popping your p's." Maybe you've seen those round screens clamped onto mics in front of a singer's or reader's mouth in recording studios? Those are to help diffuse the effect of explosions of air caused by enthusiastic "p" sounds coming from the artist. For the most part, in a church setting, keeping the mic at an appropriate distance from your mouth can reduce or eliminate the "p" problem. But distracting mouth noises are always to be guarded against when you're amplified by a microphone.

On the happy upside, having microphone amplification can greatly increase your range of expression, because you can deftly use very soft volumes or louder volumes to express parts of your passage that need that touch of drama. Just carefully adjust your distance from the mic appropriately.

Always arrange for a sound check with the technicians before the service. Stand where you will be standing, and speak at the same volume(s) and intensity that you intend to use during your reading. Eliminate as many surprises as possible before the worship service begins.

What if there's no mic? In a small room, this isn't much of an issue. But if the church or hall is larger, then you will absolutely need to use your strong diaphragmatic breathing, relaxed vocal chords, clear consonant and vowel formation, and great expression. Be strong and confident. Think about your voice hitting the back wall of the room. The folks in the back need to hear the scripture just as much as the folks on the front row! Use just enough strength and energy to get your voice to the back row. Then everyone present will be able to hear and enjoy your reading.

PUTTING IT ALL TOGETHER

The Step-by-Step Process

With the theory under our belts, let's actually take a passage and work the preparation steps one at a time. See by the end if you have a much richer understanding of the text, and with it, the capacity to express it in a lively and engaging way.

STEP ONE: ANALYZE THE TEXT

Let's begin with some basic text analysis. Remember, we're not going to preach this passage; we're just going to read it with integrity. We're going to mine all the important face value stuff out of it, leaving the spiritual concepts and conclusion-drawing to the preacher. We'll take a sample passage and work through the process.

Read the passage

For this purpose, let's use **Acts 16:16–34**. Read the entire chapter through twice. This will give you a much better sense of the context of the passage. Have you got your context established? Refer to the "introduction" section of your Bible before the book of Acts, if it has one, or skip to the resource section of this book, which will give you a quick synopsis of each Bible book. As you may recall, most scholars agree that Luke wrote the book of Acts as a follow up to his first book, the Gospel of Luke. Luke accompanied Paul and his companions on the missionary journey where this event takes place. So we have Luke traveling with Paul, Timothy, and Silas, and probably others, on his second missionary journey, visiting and encouraging the young churches they established on Paul's first missionary journey. They're in the Roman colony of Philippi when the events in question take place.

Apply the text analysis checklist

We approach each passage with our quick checklist to get our bearings:

1. Read the text, perhaps in a couple of different translations.

2. Read it again—what did you miss?

3. Back up a few paragraphs and get the context.

4. Why did Luke tell this story?

5. Jot down the main events.

6. Refer to a Bible commentary or your study Bible notes if you need help.

Now, Luke relates quite an amazing adventure story in this passage. Can you retell the story from memory, not leaving out any important details? Write it out in your own words—list the events as bullet points if that helps. Now check that against the text. What important plot points did you miss? This example from Acts is an exciting narrative, so we have one event leading to the next in a linear fashion. We can see the domino effect of each plot point on the next. This part of the process will be a bit different for, say, one of Paul's letters where he is explaining a theological concept. In that case, we would list the points of Paul's theological arguments as one builds on another to make his point.

Let's take our passage step-by-step. In the first words of the Acts passage, we learn that Luke actually was present in this story; he was an eyewitness to this event ("As **we** were going to the place of prayer . . . " vs. 16). This gives the passage a sense of immediacy. This is not just something Luke heard about—he saw it happen with his own eyes. So, how would we list the key events? Here's my quick bullet list:

- Paul and companions meet a fortune-telling slave girl

- She loudly identifies them as "servants of the Most High God"

- This continued for days

- Paul, exasperated, casts out the demon from the slave girl

- The girl's owners, now with no way to make money, drag Paul and Silas to the magistrates

- The slave owners accuse Paul and Silas of unlawful behavior

- The magistrates have Paul and Silas beaten and imprisoned

- The magistrates warn the jailer not to let anything happen to the prisoners

- At midnight, an earthquake shakes the foundations of the prison and causes the doors to open

- Assuming the prisoners had escaped, the jailer prepares to take his own life

- Paul stops the jailer, assuring him that no prisoners had escaped

- Overcome with relief, the jailer asks Paul, "What must I do to be saved?"

- Paul responds, "Believe in the Lord Jesus, and you will be saved, you and your household."

- The jailer takes them into his house and feeds them and bandages their wounds

- The jailer's entire household believes and is baptized.

Now we can see the flow of the story and pull out some highlights. We can immediately see the dramatic potential of this passage: casting out demons, beatings, earthquakes, near-suicide, mass conversion to Christianity! And don't miss the surprise plot twist that happens when Paul and Silas DON'T escape once the prison doors are thrown wide! This unexpected turn of events results in the jailer and his family coming to trust the Lord. Huzzah—happy ending!

STEP TWO: CREATE YOUR VISUAL ROAD MAP

Type the passage

OK, time to mark your text and map out your oratory game plan. You can type the passage by copying it out of your physical Bible, or, to make it easier for yourself, go to Biblegateway.com, choose the preferred translation, and then cut and paste the text into a Google doc or Word doc. Double- or triple-space the reading to make room for notes. If you love color, this is the time to get out your markers or colored pencils.

Mark the passage

This is just about my favorite part of the process because this is where I get to make a lot of artistic decisions. Here are some of the things you're looking for:

- What is the general flow and pacing of the reading?

- What parts need to be slower and deliberate so that the listeners can catch important details?

- Which parts should be sped up a bit to highlight the urgency or drama?

- What are the characters feeling or experiencing?

- What specific words or contrasts need to be emphasized so that the meaning of the sentence is clear?

- Are there any words that the writer repeats for emphasis?

- What colorful words stand out?

- Where will pauses help or hurt the dramatic flow?

- Is this passage sad, happy, exciting, foreboding, stern, encouraging, or some combination of these?

- Are there any awkward phrases or hard-to-pronounce words that need some focused rehearsal so that they don't trip you up in the moment?

PUTTING IT ALL TOGETHER

Here is how my version of this passage might look, once I've marked it up to my liking:

Acts 16:16-34 English Standard Version (ESV)

~~Paul and Silas in Prison~~

(16 As we were going to the place of prayer, we were met by a <u>slave girl</u> who had a <u>spirit of divination</u> and brought her owners <u>much gain</u> by <u>fortune-telling</u>. 17 She followed Paul and us, crying out, "These men are servants of the <u>Most High God</u>, who proclaim to you <u>the way of salvation</u>." 18 And this she kept doing for many days. Paul, having become greatly <u>annoyed</u>, turned and said to the spirit, "<u>I command you</u> in the <u>name of Jesus</u> Christ to <u>come out of her</u>." And it came out <u>that very hour</u>.

19 But when her owners saw that their <u>hope of gain</u> was gone, they <u>seized</u> Paul and Silas and <u>dragged</u> them into the marketplace before the rulers. 20 And when they had brought them to the <u>magistrates</u>, they said, "These men are <u>Jews</u>, and they are <u>disturbing our city</u>. 21 They advocate <u>customs</u> that are not lawful for us as <u>Romans</u> to accept or practice." 22 The crowd joined in <u>attacking them</u>, and the magistrates <u>tore</u> the garments off them and gave orders to <u>beat them with rods</u>. 23 And when they had <u>inflicted many blows</u> upon them, they <u>threw them</u> into prison, ordering the jailer to keep them <u>safely</u>. 24 Having received this order, he put them into the <u>inner prison</u> and fastened their <u>feet in the stocks</u>. //

②

~~The Philippian Jailer Converted~~

(25 About midnight) Paul and Silas were praying and singing hymns to God,
and the prisoners were listening to them, 26 and suddenly there was a great
earthquake, so that the foundations of the prison were shaken. And
immediately all the doors were opened, and everyone's bonds were
unfastened. 27 When the jailer woke and saw that the prison doors were
open, he drew his sword and was about to kill himself, supposing that the
prisoners had escaped. 28 But Paul cried with a loud voice, "Do not harm
yourself, for we are all here." 29 And the jailer called for lights and rushed in,
and trembling with fear he fell down before Paul and Silas. 30 Then he
brought them out and said, "Sirs, what must I do to be saved?" 31 And they
said // Believe in the Lord Jesus, and you will be saved, you and your
household. 32 And they spoke the word of the Lord to him and to all who
were in his house. 33 And he took them the same hour of the night and
washed their wounds; and he was baptized at once, he and all his family. 34
Then he brought them up into his house and set food before them. And he
rejoiced along with his entire household that he had believed in God. //

The Word of the Lord.

STEP THREE: PRACTICE THE PASSAGE OUT LOUD

I know you may be tempted to skip this part, but do yourself a huge favor, and do it. *Reading out loud is nothing at all like reading in your head.* Don't count on being able to turn your marked text into a finely executed reading the very first time it's out of your mouth, in front of people. Practice. I know you may feel awkward, but it's so much better to be awkward in the privacy of your own home, alone, or with a loved one than up in front of the whole congregation. And you owe it to them to give them the best possible oration of the passage. You can expect many benefits from reading out loud:

- You'll get used to the words. Some combinations of words are just awkward to get out correctly the first time you do it. Practicing out loud lets you know where those places are and points out where you need to drill down a bit. Repeat the phrase four to five times until words flow easily.

- You'll understand the flow of the story and learn where the ups and downs of the narrative or the rhetorical argument go. This will help you know what should be emphasized to make the best sense of the reading.

- You'll know how much is enough and how much is too much. Practice moderating the amount of expression needed to appropriately tell the story. When you read out loud several times, you can try out different styles and amounts of expression until you settle on just the right amount to get the job done without going over the top.

- You can get feedback from someone you trust. None of us is objective enough to really evaluate ourselves, so having someone available to offer constructive criticism is a valuable asset. Ask him if he understood the reading, if he got the main points, or if any areas were confusing. Slow down those sections and take the time to let your hearers absorb the meaning. Did you enunciate clearly? Could you be heard at a distance—were you supporting your voice from your diaphragm? How was your eye contact? Your friendly audience can help by checking you in these areas.

The goal is for your hearers to stop looking at you, and start watching the story unfold in their imaginations as they listen.

STEP FOUR: DELIVER THE TEXT

What is your prayer for the congregation as they hear this passage? Take some time and actually pray for yourself, your congregation, and the others that will be serving in the worship service.

Pre-reading checklist

1. Are you dressed properly?

2. Are you generally hydrated?

3. Have you been to the restroom lately? (Do we need to have a discussion about what adrenaline does to your bladder?)

4. Did you get a good night's sleep last night?

5. Can you do a little deep breathing to relax?

6. Are you feeling unhurried or rushed, and if so, what will help you slow down and focus?

7. Do you need a bottle of water for a quick sip before you read?

8. Are you reading out of a pulpit Bible or from your own marked notes?

9. If using the pulpit Bible, is the passage clearly marked? If using your notes, will you keep them with you until you read, or place them on the lectern to be used at the appropriate time?

10. If your notes are several pages long, are the page numbers clearly marked? This is critical insurance in case your papers fall to the floor and get shuffled out of order.

11. Are there any obstacles for you as you move to your reading position (chairs, cords, flower arrangements, etc.)?

Tech check

1. Have you tested the mic with the sound tech?

2. Are any recording devices working properly?

3. Is the lighting sufficient to easily see your text?

Great! Let's prepare to read! Remember, it's not about you. God's got this. It's his job to touch the hearts in the congregation. Just do what you practiced and enjoy the opportunity!

OTHER IMPORTANT DETAILS

A Quick Note on Vestments and Licensing

VESTMENTS

In some churches the tradition calls for the lay readers to wear robes, usually plain white albs, when they serve in the altar party (the group of lay people and clergy members officiating at the front of the church). Other churches are more casual and do not ask lay readers to vest or even take part as a member of the altar party; the readers simply move from their place in the congregation to the lectern when the time comes for the readings. Either way is perfectly acceptable, as your parish prefers.

But why vestments at all?

The traditional purpose of vestments, for clergy of any rank and for lay ministers, is to cover the individuality of the person and point to the ministry. When vested, we cease making statements about ourselves with our appearance and we take on a neutral appearance, which then allows our ministry, our role, to take center stage. Vestments do not signify superiority over other lay people; rather, they should signify servanthood. The alb can remind us that we are no longer representing ourselves, but our specific ministry in the context of worship. This idea pairs nicely with our mission as lay readers to put our full focus on expressing the word of God with integrity.

LICENSING

The role of lay reader doesn't require ordination—that's why we're called *lay* readers. We link the laity in the pews with the clergy. We read the scriptures and, in the absence of a Deacon, also the Prayers of the People as the people's representatives. But we should be expected to demonstrate some competency in handling our responsibilities. Some dioceses do require actual licensing for lay readers, which is a process meant to ensure competence in liturgical knowledge and practice, but this requirement is far from universal. Many, many churches only ask for volunteers willing to serve. Check with your local church about their requirements, and take advantage of any training offered.

RESOURCES

PREPARING
THROUGH PRAYER

As we come to our preparation of a text or the reading of the scripture passages on a Sunday morning, please remember who this is all really about: God and your listeners. It is not about you. You're not there to impress anyone or show off. You're there to serve. I urge you to pray to God that your reading of his word will help your congregation and further the kingdom of heaven. I've jotted down a few ideas for you to use or modify, as you like:

"Heavenly Father, thank you for the gift of your word—your revelation of yourself through the ages. I pray that you will open my eyes to your truth, wisdom, and love for your people through your Son, Jesus Christ. Help me express your words in a way that brings life to your people. You tell us that your word will accomplish what you sent it out to do—accomplish that will through this reading. Amen."

"Abba Father, show me the areas of my life that need to be adjusted, changed, or put to death. Please use this passage to help me grow in conformity to the example of Christ. It is only by your power that I can hope to become more and more holy. Because you are a God who uses the weak rather than the strong, and the humble rather than the proud, I pray you will use me to share your word with this congregation today. Amen."

"Good Lord, as I study your word, I ask that you show me why you caused it to be written. Help me study and understand your purposes in this text. Help me communicate your exhortation and encouragement for your dearly loved congregation here today. Your word is a light to our paths and a lamp to our feet (Psalm 119:105). Give us the strength to walk in it. Amen."

"Our Father, thank you for the opportunity to share your word with my congregation today. I pray that you use this reading to grow the faith of these people who hear your word. You tell us in Romans, 'Faith comes from hearing, and hearing through the word of Christ' (Romans 10:17). Let these worshipers hear you speak to them through this passage. Amen."

BIBLE BOOK THEMES

L et's take a look at each book of the Bible, in order, and talk about how its role in the biblical arc might affect the way we read it out loud.

OLD TESTAMENT

Many people are wary of the Old Testament because so many of the stories are dark, violent, confusing, and seemingly outdated. It is old. The beginning of God's story came a long time ago. But as we'll see, the Old Testament contains a deliberate arc and a continuity that must be studied and grasped to fully appreciate the meta story of God's relationship with people and our response to him. Ignorance of the Old Testament will severely hinder one's understanding of the New Testament. In fact, only twelve chapters of the New Testament *do not* quote the Old Testament. It's that critical.

Pentateuch (from the Greek for "five volumes")—the First Five Books:

Also known as the "Torah," or "law" in Hebrew, the books of the Pentateuch lay the foundation for all of scripture that follows. Establishing God's identity and his purpose for creating everything with the Hebrews as his chosen people, teaching all people his character and his ways, the events of these five books set the stage for the story of the fall and ultimate redemption, though that perfect redemption is only foreshadowed in these early books. The true fulfillment of God's plan comes in the life, death, and resurrection of Jesus, but God begins instructing his people about how things work from the earliest times. The authorship of Genesis is traditionally attributed to Moses, though scholars speculate that it was completed by contemporaries and subsequent followers. The audience, then, was the Hebrew people coming out of Egypt and into the promised land. Watch for the critical theme of "covenant," where God promises lots of amazing things in return for obeying and following him. Also notice how humanity continues to fall desperately short on our part of the covenant, or contract.

Genesis: The beginning of everything. Genesis recounts the creation of the cosmos and everything in it, including people. We see the beginning of man's (meaning humanity's) relationship with God, how it began in perfect unity and was then broken by the sin of Adam and Eve. And so began the cycle of men doing evil, God disciplining his chosen people, men repenting and enjoying a short time of peace, men doing evil and forgetting or rebelling against God's law, God disciplining them and restoring them, and around it goes. In Genesis we meet Adam and Eve, Abraham, Isaac, and Jacob. In Genesis we're introduced to the foundational concept of "covenant," where God makes a "contract" with Abraham. God promises to make Abraham a great nation, to give him a special place to dwell, to bless all nations through him, and to be present with the people in tangible ways. This book contains a lot of history that sets the stage for the books to follow. It contains many of the familiar Bible stories we may have learned as kids.

Exodus: This second of the Pentateuch books continues the story of God's plan unfolding, the amazing expansion of the Hebrew people in Egypt with the rise of Joseph to power, Pharaoh coming to despise and oppress the Hebrews, and the rise of Moses, who leads the Hebrew people out of slavery to the Egyptians. Once out of Egypt and into the desert, the Lord, through Moses, hands down the Ten Commandments, and teaches the people about holiness, as they build an earthly home for God's presence in the tabernacle. God shows himself to the people in fire and cloud as he leads them through the desert. But still, they cannot obey their faithful God. Exodus clearly shows man's inability to follow God's instruction, even in the face of miracles and blessings. The people continue to rebel and reject God. God continues to mete out justice, forgive, and lead the people forward again.

Leviticus: This book is a continuation of the book of Exodus, as it was written quickly after the completion of the tabernacle. This is the book which gets a bad rap as being a boring bunch of weird laws and lists. These lists focus on describing what is holy and what is not holy in the eyes of God. In fact, this book is very instructional in the basic Christian concept of atonement, the paying for and removing of sin. God is dead serious about purity and holiness. The ritual and ethical laws in this book told the Hebrew people, and us, how important purity is to God, and what it takes to be holy. A lot of the rules in Leviticus sound strange and baffling to our twenty-first century minds, but with some historical context and an eye to the broader spiritual purpose, it becomes clear to see how God was specifically calling the Hebrew people to be a peculiar people "set apart" from all other people groups to know and serve him.

Numbers: As the name implies, Numbers has lots of numbers in it. The narrative story occasionally breaks into a report of census taking and law giving. But those laws are important, and the narrative is pretty exciting: full of battles, rebellion, retribution, miracles and intrigue. Again, God is teaching the Hebrew people how to follow him faithfully. He continues to make good on his end of the covenant, leading them to the promised land of Canaan. In this book we hear the famous story about the cowardly spies that Joshua sent into the land—though the land was just as God had promised, flowing with milk and honey, the spies also reported the presence of giants, and the people were too fearful to go in to take the land. God sent them back into the desert to wander for forty more years.

Deuteronomy: This last book of the Pentateuch records Moses's last big speeches to the Hebrews, recounting the faithfulness of God in the face of the unfaithfulness of the Hebrew people, Moses's commissioning of Joshua to lead the people, and his final exhortation before he dies. This book is quoted extensively in the New Testament, especially by Jesus and Paul.

Historical Books

I don't want to move forward without making this important point: Christianity (and of course, Judaism) is a faith grounded in history. Ours is not just a collection of untethered "dos and don'ts" scribed by a single person who got a flash of inspiration designed to be applied in some kind of generally spiritual way. No. Rather, God demonstrates in particular places and times, his sovereign nature, his divine purpose, and his steadfast love for his people, by acting in profound ways through the lives of notable people throughout history. This sets us apart as serving a God who has come into our human condition—rooted in space and time—and revealed himself through the lives of many men and women who were weak, flawed and prone to spectacular failure. I hope this gives you pause, and that you take great encouragement from it. Through history, God repeatedly demonstrates both his love for his wayward creation and his ability to restore it to wholeness.

The next dozen books of the Bible are called the "historical books" as they recount the major milestones in the history of the Israelites, a span of about 1,000 years. Each book underscores the main themes of the Bible: God's promises, his faithfulness to fulfill his promises, man's repeated unfaithfulness, God's judgment and reconciliation, and the longing for the ultimate fulfillment of his covenant with Abraham. Major plot points of Israelite history during this period include Israel's entry into the promised land, the rise of the twelve judges (civil/military leaders), the division of

Israel into two competing kingdoms—larger Israel in the north and smaller Judah in the south, the downward spiral of both of these kingdoms, their exile into pagan kingdoms, and Judah's return to its former homeland.

Joshua: Joshua completes Moses's mandate and brings the people into the land God promised to Abraham. He leads the people into battles with the Canaanites and defeats them. He leads the people in the famous, unorthodox battle of Jericho, where "the walls come atumblin' down," in the words of the famous song. God continues to rout out betrayal and unfaithfulness in the ranks, divides the promised land among the Hebrew tribes, and brings the land into unity under his sovereign reign. Joshua's name foreshadows the coming of Christ, as both the names Joshua and Jesus derive from the Hebrew word meaning "God saves."

Judges: After the death of Joshua, things got pretty dicey in the history of the Israelites. The people fell away from God and worshipped pagan idols. Then, God raised up a series of twelve judges to rule the people, and for the most part, when a judge was at the helm, the people did alright. But when the judge died, the people messed up again, in big ways. And sadly, the judges themselves devolved from the first judge to the last. Not all the judges get much ink in the story. Notable are Deborah (a pretty good judge and good leader in war); Gideon, who started weak, became strong and then got way too full of himself; Abimelech, a king who was rotten from the get-go; Jephthah, inept and corrupt; and finally, Samson, who was, as leaders go, a loose cannon and often quite a fool. In the book of Judges, we see the repeated refrain, "And the people of Israel did what was evil in the sight of the Lord." The nation was rife with corruption, civil war, and chaos. With very few sparks of light to break it up, this was a dark time for God's chosen people.

Ruth: The author is unknown. But the book tells a profound love story that takes place during the time of the judges and stars two women, the older Israelite, Naomi, and the younger, Ruth, a foreigner from Moab. A mother and her daughter-in-law return to Israel from Moab because their husbands have died and they seek the safety of community to survive. Boaz, a relative of Naomi's, provides work and sustenance by offering Ruth a job gleaning in his fields. Naomi devises a plan to get Ruth into Boaz's good graces. Boaz is very much taken with Ruth and offers to marry her. He becomes her "kinsman redeemer," foreshadowing the redemption of God's people by Jesus himself. This is no "once upon a time" fairy tale. Ruth and Boaz are rooted in history and eventually become the grandparents of the great King David, and the many-times great grandparents of Jesus.

1 and 2 Samuel: These books take the name of an important priest and prophet, who is instrumental in transitioning Israel from the governance of judges to the anointing of its first earthly king. Samuel anoints a tall, handsome man named Saul as king of Israel, but predictably, Saul's reign begins to break down as a result of his growing self-reliance and disobedience to God's decrees. Samuel then anoints David as king while he is still just a humble shepherd boy. Through Samuel, God not only makes David the king, but promises that through the line of David, the Messiah will come to rule and reign forever. In 1 Samuel, we read one of the all-time favorite stories of the Bible: the young man David defeats the huge warrior Goliath with just a stone and a slingshot, sending the humiliated Philistine army running for their lives. But David not only must wait for Saul to die before he can become king, but Saul spends years jealously pursuing David, bent on killing him. David is unwavering in his commitment not to kill Saul, even when he gets the chance, and only takes the throne once Saul ultimately brings his own death down on himself. The story of David and his kingdom continues in 2 Samuel and chronicles his military victories and the establishment of Jerusalem as the City of David. Unfortunately, even as David is a "man after God's own heart," he too falls prey to natural temptation and sin. We read the tragic stories of David's lusting for Bathsheba, his adultery with her, and the murder of her husband in the attempted cover-up. The prophet Nathan confronts David, bringing him to repentance. His relationship with God is restored, but there is a steep price to pay. His kingdom and his own children are wracked with conflict and betrayal, violence and death. But God keeps his promise to David and the Davidic line becomes the family tree of Jesus.

1 and 2 Kings: These two books describe the period of monarchs in Israel from about 970–586 BC, beginning with Solomon's rise to power upon the death of David, the building of the temple, and Solomon's wisdom and success turning slowly into apostasy and ruin. Subsequent kings continue to fail to follow God's law, resulting in the division of the kingdom into Judah in the south and Israel in the north. Both of these kingdoms are carried off into exile, and Jerusalem and the holy temple are destroyed. But hope is not lost—the line of kings does not end with the destruction of David's city. Jesus, the ultimate king, has yet to come on the scene. The authorship of these two books is debated by scholars, with many suggesting the prophet Jeremiah, but it is clear that the author relied heavily on the book of Deuteronomy in the way he holds the kings of this period up to scrutiny.

1 Chronicles and 2 Chronicles: The books of Chronicles cover a lot of the same time periods as Samuel and Kings and contain common stories. The books of Chronicles emphasize the importance of the Davidic line of kings and focus on the history of Judah, the southern kingdom, through the exile in Babylon and the destruction of Jerusalem and the temple. But on a hopeful note seventy years later, 2 Chronicles ends with the decree from Cyrus, King of Persia, to rebuild the temple, a sign that God had not abandoned his people.

Ezra and Nehemiah: Jewish tradition held that the same author was responsible for both the books of Nehemiah and Ezra and the two books were counted as one. They both contain similar information to the books of Chronicles but with slightly different thrusts. Significantly, Chronicles gives King Solomon a much more positive treatment, whereas Ezra and Nehemiah are critical of his intermarriage with foreign cultures, leading to his ultimate downfall. Both Ezra and Nehemiah try to demonstrate God's faithfulness and his working out of his sovereign plan in the rebuilding of the temple and in restoring the Jewish exiles after the Babylonian captivity.

Esther: This book recounts the origin of the Jewish festival of Purim, which has a lot of popular appeal. The story's namesake, Ester, was a young Jewish girl who found herself married to the king of Persia when his first wife did not toe the line. It's an exciting tale of bravery, intrigue, and revenge, ending in the saving of the Jewish people from extermination. This book, though somewhat controversial, has always been a part of the Jewish canon despite never mentioning God. Though he is never mentioned *per se*, God's providence is seen operating on behalf of his people. This book's author is unknown, and it is only speculatively dated, perhaps about 486–464 BC.

Poetry and Wisdom Literature

Poetic literature in the Bible is not limited to the next five books, but it is most dramatically displayed in them. Unfortunately the beauty and complexity of this poetry does not always survive the translation from the original Hebrew to our English versions. Because few of us read Hebrew, we miss the beautiful acrostic psalms, the alliteration of the words and syllables, and the plays on words that characterize these books. We can see some evidence of recognizable poetry in the arrangement of the lines and the parallel couplets of many psalms and proverbs. The "wisdom" literature in the Old Testament is generally characterized as those books that either state specifically certain ways of living as the best paths forward, or they wrestle with challenging issues in life and how to deal with them.

Job: This ancient book gives few clues to its authorship except we know from his descriptions and vocabulary that he was well traveled and well educated. This story, through its title character, wrestles with the universal question regarding suffering, specifically, how do people like us who look to a personal God deal with the balance of sovereignty, justice, and mercy? Job's wife and three friends offer flawed arguments which fail in the eyes of God. Throughout, Job remains perplexed, yet faithful and trusting, declaring "I know that my Redeemer lives."

Psalms: The Psalms contain many of the most quoted and memorized scripture verses in the whole of the Bible. These songs and poems resonate with us because they reflect the gamut of human emotions, from joy and praise to anger and despair. We go to the Psalms for comfort and encouragement because the psalmists understood and expressed those feelings so beautifully. These poem-songs give us permission to speak to God from our hearts, even when those hearts are black with fear or hate or even bald-faced presumption. Almost all of the Psalms end in praise to God regardless of how angrily they may begin. It seems that the very act of airing our pain helps us work back around to trust in God's enduring love and faithfulness. King David wrote almost half of the psalms (73 of the 150 psalms), along with the Sons of Korah, Solomon, and even Moses. Many psalms have no author attributed to them.

Proverbs: Scholars date the writing of this book to the time of Solomon and attribute the authorship, or at least the curation of these proverbial sayings, to him. The proverbs cover a wide range of everyday situations and offer the best options for godly living in the face of those situations. The "fear of the Lord" motivates the author to advise one course of action over another in practical matters of family and community life. The goal of pleasing God is often the unspoken standard in making those choices. In modern times, these proverbs are often misconstrued as "promises" of God. However, they make no such claim. Rather, they are common sense pronouncements of what kind of life choices will most likely bring happiness and harmony to one's life.

Ecclesiastes: Scholars are divided about the authorship of Ecclesiastes—some attributing it to King Solomon and others finding reason to date the book much later in history. In any case, this book is quite unique in its perspective. No purveyor of pat answers, this author asks provocative and challenging questions in his journey to figure out the meaning of life. He responds to dozens of instances of futility and injustice with the repeated refrain "All is vanity." On the other hand, he finds joy and beauty in the world around him. Because all indeed is vanity, he points to trust in God as the only way to avoid the futility of life that aggravates him on all other fronts. God's work and character are enduring and not subject to change or contingent on earthly circumstances.

Song of Solomon: Again, this book's authorship is in question by scholars, its name notwithstanding. Some say that its so-called attribution in Chapter 1:1 ("The Song of Songs, which is Solomon's") just means that it was written *for* Solomon and not necessarily *by* him. In any case, this is a magnificent piece of love poetry describing the romantic relationship between a young man and a young woman. Several different interpretive theories have emerged: The poem is an analogy for the relationship between God and his people, or it's analogous to the relationship between Christ and his church. Still others just see it as a celebration of covenantal love and mutual enjoyment found in the confines of godly marriage. In any case, the Song of Solomon, or Song of Songs, is a feast of sensual imagery and lyric expression.

Prophetic Books

Though prophets were active in Israel's history much earlier, the writings of prophets didn't appear until the eighth century BC. We have records of the lives and ministries of Abraham, Nathan, and Samuel, for example, but they did not write down their words of exhortation into any specific volumes. The job of a prophet was very specific: he had to speak words given to him directly by God, he must never encourage the people to follow any other gods but Yahweh, and his predictive announcements must *always* come true. If any of these conditions did not hold, the prophet was considered false, and punishment was swift. "Repent and return to the Lord," was the most common message of the prophets, as the people continually drifted into apostasy. Sometimes the message was one of hope, as the oppressed people longed for relief from oppression and for their ultimate King and Messiah. The prophets, bringing unwelcome news of God's displeasure, lived difficult lives bearing the burden of the people's transgressions and tasked with calling them back to God-honoring lifestyles. Most died as martyrs at the hands of those they were trying to help or by oppressive rulers who were threatened by the prophet's message.

Major Prophets

Isaiah: Arguably the greatest prophet of Israel was Isaiah who wrote his beautiful tome over the course of about fifty years. (As with many Old Testament books, scholars speculate that Isaiah didn't write *all* of the book bearing his name, but for our purposes, we will assume he was the writer.) His writing is poetic and full of allusion and vision. Isaiah prophesied to the nation through a tumultuous time in its history, through the fall of Israel and the sustaining of the kingdom of Judah as a remnant. Isaiah challenges the Jews to live in the hope of God's fulfilled promises of the coming Messiah. Of particular interest to lay readers, Isaiah's vision of God's throne room in Chapter 6 comes up in the Lectionary with some frequency. Also of note is Isaiah 52–53, a passage which clearly foretells many details of the life, death, and resurrection of Jesus the Christ.

Jeremiah: Jeremiah prophesied to the southern tribe of Judah also, nearly a century after Isaiah, during the years before the tribe of Judah was taken into captivity, warning them to return to the Lord to avoid his judgment. Then, in the midst of that captivity, he encouraged them to remain true to the living God, reminding them in God's own words that he had not forsaken his promise to ultimately save his people. Jeremiah's most oft-quoted pronouncement from the Lord "'For I know the plans I have for you,' declares the Lord, 'plans for welfare and not for evil, to give you a future and a hope,'" (Chapter 29:11) assures the people that in the midst of their suffering, God is still in control and working the events of history to ultimately bring victory and peace to the kingdom of God.

Lamentations: Again, the authorship of Lamentations is up for grabs, as there is no indication in the text of who wrote it. Was it Jeremiah or was it a committee of others? We don't know. But scholars agree that its theology and theme align with the Old Testament law, describing events in an eyewitness style that coincide with Jeremiah's experience. Lamentations was written to be prayed and sung during the period before the temple was destroyed, in the desolate time after its destruction, and during the time of rebuilding. It continued to form the spiritual framework for prayers and songs used on those occasions that the people remembered that dark time in their history. Lamentations offers confession of sin, expressions of hope, and acknowledges total dependence on God.

Ezekiel: Ezekiel's ministry during the Babylonian captivity overlapped the ministry of Jeremiah, so his audience was very similar. His stern pronouncements of judgment on the unfaithful people of God are balanced by his message of restoration that God was going to bring to Judah, not because the people had earned it, but because of his own merciful nature, for his own name's sake. Ezekiel incessantly calls on the people of Israel to repent and return to the Lord, to be restored to a right relationship with him. Ezekiel's prophetic oracles are usually framed at the beginning and end by the bookends of "The word of the Lord came to me . . ." and "They shall know that I am the Lord." Thanks to the children's song, most of us have heard of Ezekiel's vision of a "wheel in a wheel, way up in the middle of the air," where God entrusted Ezekiel to go speak his words to the hardhearted people of Israel.

Daniel: The book of Daniel was ostensibly written by the young man Daniel during the time of the Babylonian exile. Daniel had come from a high-ranking home and was chosen with three of his friends to serve in the court of Nebuchadnezzar, because of his wisdom and his ability as a "seer." In spite of heavy pressure to cave to this new pagan culture, Daniel and his friends remained faithful to the one true God. In Daniel we read the story of Shadrach, Meshach, and Abednego surviving the punishment of the fiery furnace, with God himself as their companion. In the book of Daniel, we find the story of the dreaded "handwriting on the wall," the pronouncement of God's judgment on the foolish Babylonian king. We also read about how Daniel is thrown to the lions because of his devotion to prayer and worship of Yahweh, yet he survives by God's miraculous intervention. After the chronicles of Daniel's life in Babylon, the book turns to Daniel's prophetic visions. Especially noteworthy are Daniel's foretelling of the coming of the Christ, the "Son of Man." Jesus told the authorities and crowds at his trial that *he* is the Son of Man in Daniel's visions, echoing Daniel's words: "But I tell you, from now on you will see the Son of Man seated at the right hand of Power and coming on the clouds of heaven" (*Matthew 29:64*). The high priest tore his robes in anger at Jesus claiming to be the divine character spoken of in these well-known Old Testament prophecies.

Minor Prophets

Minor prophets are only distinguished from major prophets because of the length of the books themselves, not because their message carries any less weight. The universal theme of all of God's prophets has been largely the same through the ages, with some variation to address specific audiences and circumstances: Repent. Turn back to the Lord. Save yourselves from the coming judgment. Nevertheless, the Lord will save you because of his steadfast love, to fulfill his promises to the patriarchs, and for his own name's sake before the nations. We will quickly touch on each of the minor prophets to highlight their unique circumstances.

Hosea: Hosea was a prophet to the northern kingdom of Israel, well before the Babylonian exile, but at a time of great political upheaval. Not only did that kingdom turn over six kings in thirty years, but the people were heavily influenced by the surrounding pagan culture which worshipped Baal. This bloodthirsty agricultural deity's devotees were seeped in every kind of evil practice one might imagine. Hosea had his work cut out for him, but he never gave up, reminding the Israelites that they were indeed the people of Yahweh.

Joel: Scholars have not nailed down exactly when the book of Joel was written, but based on the events the book describes, they suggest a large range of time from the ninth to the fourth centuries. God's call through Joel for the people to repent and acknowledge the Lord in their midst, as with other prophets, are central ideas. Joel also famously promises the outpouring of God's spirit in the last days, "And it shall come to pass afterward, that I will pour out my Spirit on all flesh; your sons and your daughters shall prophesy, your old men shall dream dreams, and your young men shall see visions. Even on the male and female servants in those days I will pour out my Spirit" *(Joel 2:28–29)*.

Amos: Amos wasn't a professional prophet exactly, but a shepherd that God had chosen to bring a message of judgment to the northern kingdom of Israel. Though he begins his pronouncements of judgment on the neighbors of Israel and Judah, he soon turns on God's people themselves, leveling God's accusations of unfaithfulness and rebellion.

Obadiah: In this short prophetic vision, coming to the people of Judah during the fall of Jerusalem, the writer condemns the conquering nation of Edom for its abuse of God's people and comforts the people of Judah who have experienced extreme hardship at Edom's hands. Obadiah brings hope to these people that God is still in control and working his plan to bring ultimate peace to his people.

Jonah: The book of Jonah is named for its main character, a prophet who served between 782 and 753 BC. Jonah, ironically, is held up as a character *not* to be emulated. In contrast to God's compassionate nature, Jonah worked very hard to avoid preaching God's saving message to the pagan country of Nineveh. Not only did Jonah flatly disobey God, he refused to extend the grace of God to the Ninevites that God himself showed. When Jonah relented and finally preached to the people of Nineveh, they repented and turned to the Lord. Jonah's surprising reaction to this sincere repentance was disappointment that he wouldn't get to see the Ninevites annihilated. Message: God's mercy and compassion for all of his creation is infinitely higher than ours; our judgment is selfish and ungodly. Don't be like Jonah.

Micah: Micah was a contemporary of Isaiah's, speaking to the people of Judah with much the same message as the prophets of his day, namely, that they were transgressing against Yahweh and that judgment in the form of armies from Assyria were poised against them. Micah spoke in lyrical form, using symbol and allegory, but his message was straightforward: repent and receive the mercy and blessing of the Almighty God. The most familiar verse from Micah is "He has told you, O man, what is good; and what does the Lord require of you but to do justice, and to love kindness, and to walk humbly with your God?" (6:8).

Nahum: This prophet has a single message of woe to one of Judah's enemies—the city of Nineveh, the capital of Assyria. Yes, the Ninevites had repented as a result of the preaching of Jonah, but a hundred years later, they had forgotten God's mercy and turned again to plundering Israel. The book of Nahum has been dubbed "war poetry" because of its verse construction and its almost eyewitness-style account of the hostile destruction to come. As Nahum predicted, Nineveh fell to Babylon in 612 BC, never to be rebuilt.

Habakkuk: The prophet Habakkuk never addressed the people of Israel as most prophets did. In contrast, the book consists of conversations between himself and God. Habakkuk, in the midst of a political turmoil in Israel, questions God's love for his people in the face of decades of suffering. Like the writer of Job, this prophet struggles to understand how God's justice works. How could he allow a more evil nation to be used as the instrument to chasten a less evil nation? God replies that both nations are guilty and will be equitably judged. He assures Habakkuk that his sovereign will and love of Israel will prevail. This news transformed the prophet from a confused and frustrated man to one fully trusting in God's unshakable character.

Zephaniah: The prophet Zephaniah preached during the reign of one of Judah's "good" kings, Josiah. Though Josiah did a good job reforming Judah and reinstating the observance of the mandated Jewish feasts, not all of Judah was so reformed. Zephaniah, like many other prophets, focused on two main points: the wicked will be judged "on the day of the Lord" and the righteous will be saved.

Haggai: Haggai's writing came in the year 520 BC, after the return of the exiles from Babylon. The ruler of the time, Cyrus, had opened the door for the people to begin rebuilding the temple, but their energy and enthusiasm had waned. Haggai's mission was to reignite the people to the purposeful, intentional rebuilding effort as a way to show their renewed devotion to God. The physical building process doubled as an analogy for the people rededicating themselves to serving Yahweh alone, and paving the way for the royal Davidic line to eventually find its fulfillment in Christ.

Zechariah: The prophet Zechariah, a contemporary of Haggai, related apocalyptic visions that have much in common with the style in the book of Revelation, written by the Apostle John at the end of the New Testament. An angel accompanied Zechariah through several quick and disjointed dream-visions full of symbols that the angel explained to him. Most relate to the restoring of Israel to her former glory by God's mercy and power. God promised to judge Israel's enemies and restore faithful leadership to her, replacing shepherds who have scattered the sheep and taken advantage of them. Hundreds of years later, Jesus alluded to this prophecy as he called himself the Good Shepherd who cares sacrificially for his sheep.

Malachi: The prophet Malachi was a contemporary of Ezra and Nehemiah, evidenced by his mention of similar events in history and similar complaints against the people of Israel. He wrote about eighty years after the rebuilding of the temple in Zechariah's time when the people had grown complacent and morally sloppy. He structured the narrative as an imaginary conversation between God and the Jewish people in which God makes accusations and the people ask, "How is this so?" God responds with example after example of the people's faithlessness toward him. Israel is warned to remember the Law of Moses and the coming day of the Lord.

The Apocrypha

These "intertestamental" books are received as canon (doctrinally on par with the other sixty-six books) by some denominations and not by others. In the Anglican Church, we're guided by the Thirty-Nine Articles in the matter. Article VI states: "And the other Books . . . the Church doth read for example of life and instruction of manners; but yet doth it not apply them to establish any doctrine; such are these following:

The Third Book of Esdras

The Fourth Book of Esdras

The Book of Tobias

The Book of Judith

The rest of the Book of Esther

The Book of Wisdom

Jesus the Son of Sirach

Baruch the Prophet

The Song of the Three Children

The Story of Susanna

Of Bel and the Dragon

The Prayer of Manasseh

The First Book of Maccabees

The Second Book of Maccabees"

Readings from the Apocrypha do come up in the Lectionary from time to time, so some familiarity with them is useful. Further resources regarding the Apocrypha can be found at our website: www.goodshepherdpublishing.com/eloquentlayreader/resources.

NEW TESTAMENT

The pivotal point in Christianity—in human history for that matter—was the coming of Jesus Christ, the promised Messiah. His coming ended 400 years of biblical silence and brought the news that "the kingdom of God is at hand." Many people find the New Testament to be more relatable or approachable than the Old Testament. We like the parables of Jesus and the stories of healings and miracles. But in fact, it's not possible to understand or appreciate the New Testament without the Old. Remember that one of our axioms is "context, context, context." The Old Testament is the context for the New Testament. So the two Testaments go hand in hand, with the New Testament finishing "God's story" that began in Genesis.

The Gospels and Acts (The Story of Jesus and the Early Church)

The four Gospels (meaning "good news") tell the story of Jesus's life and ministry, his trial, death, and resurrection, and they understandably contain lots of overlapping episodes. But each gospel had a specific audience and purpose, which explains the differing emphases and details contained in each. The four differing perspectives of the authors actually harmonize to paint a full and robust portrait of Jesus and his earthly life. It is in the Gospels that we hear the words of Jesus and learn most of what we know about him. In the Anglican tradition, lay people seldom get to read from the Gospels; those are usually read by the clergy. But it's important to know their role in the greater arc of the complete biblical story.

Matthew: This book is attributed almost unanimously to the apostle Matthew, one of only two original twelve disciples to write a gospel, sometime in the mid-first century. Matthew's interest was showing his fellow Jews how Jesus was the fulfillment of everything they already knew from their scriptures (the Old Testament). He begins his gospel with the genealogy of Jesus that traces his ancestry back from Abraham, through King David, tying Jesus to the well-known prophecies the Jewish people knew by heart. By the stories Matthew relates and the sermons he reports, he intends to show the people of Israel that their long-awaited Messiah had come.

Mark: Most scholars believe that the Gospel of Mark was the first gospel written, so it's not surprising that a couple of the other Gospels lean on it as a major influence. Mark, or John Mark as he was also known, was not one of the twelve disciples but a student of the apostle Peter. Featuring many of Jesus's miracles, Mark's gospel is action-packed, using the word "immediately" over and over. Mark focuses the better part of his gospel on the last week of Jesus' earthly life, culminating in his death and resurrection. Clearly to Mark, this was the most important thing to remember about Jesus.

Luke: Luke, just about universally believed to be the author of this gospel, also was not one of the twelve disciples, but a companion of Paul's, and referred to as "Luke, the beloved physician" by Paul in his letter to the Colossians (4:14). He is believed to be a Greek convert to Christianity. Covering Jesus's entire earthly life, from his birth in Bethlehem to his death on the cross and resurrection, Luke is the longest gospel, containing more accounts of Jesus's parables than any other. Luke centers his gospel on the idea that Jesus is the savior of the world who came to save the lost.

John: John's gospel differs from the first three, which are called "synoptic" Gospels because they contain many of the same stories, largely in the same order. Though an eyewitness of the events of Jesus's ministry and one of Jesus's closest friends, John focuses on seeing that both Jews and Gentiles come to understand Jesus as the Messiah who came to save all who would follow him. John calls out lots of the symbolic language Jesus used to refer to himself: the door, the vine, the good shepherd, the light of the world, the bread of life. The opening words of John Chapter 1 echo the first words of the Bible itself in Genesis: "In the beginning . . ." John humbly refers to himself in the narratives, not by name, but as "the disciple that Jesus loved." Alone among the apostles, John lived to a ripe old age and died of natural causes. There is ample reason to believe that all the others were martyred for their faith in Jesus the Christ.

Acts: This book continues the story Luke began in his gospel, written to chronicle how Christianity grew and developed, as it diverged from traditional Judaism after the death and resurrection of Jesus. The Jewish leadership rejected Christianity, rejected the notion that Jesus was the Christ, even though he had fulfilled hundreds of prophecies from the Old Testament. In Acts, we learn about the coming of the promised "helper," the Holy Spirit who would empower the early church to spread the good news of Jesus. We see the new Christians grapple with a life that was very different in many ways from their lives as Jews—a life that quite often meant persecution and even death. This book is packed with exciting stories and is a joy to read aloud. In Acts, we meet a Pharisee named Saul, hostile to Christianity, who has an earth-shattering encounter with the risen Christ. Saul converts to Christianity and becomes the faith's most traveled missionary and prolific writer. He does not actually change his name, but after his conversion, he is always referred to as Paul.

The Epistles (Letters to the Churches and Individuals)

This large collection of books were actually not books at all, but letters, written by their authors to a certain group of people to answer particular questions or address particular issues. Many of them contain some standard features of letters like a salutation, the name of the recipient, a greeting, a prayer intention for the recipient, the body of the letter, and a farewell statement. Some of these letters were personal in nature, to one recipient about one or more issues, and other epistles were clearly meant to be read and circulated among the churches of a particular region. These epistles make up the bulk of the New Testament, with Paul believed to be the author of more than any other New Testament writer.

Romans: Paul's letter to the churches in Rome, written about 54 AD, presents some challenges for the lay reader. Paul here puts forth some of his pithiest theological arguments, comparing and contrasting the role of the law and grace in the life of a believer. His audience was probably made up of both Jewish Christians and converted gentiles, as he goes into much detail about how God has unfolded his plan for salvation, balancing judgment and mercy. As a result of the detail given for these complicated concepts, the sentence structures are complicated, long and winding, full of ancillary clauses and conditions. The wise lay reader will spend a good bit of time preparing for a reading of Romans, to plan ahead for all the twists and turns of Paul's thoughtful and precise language. Do take time to work out your passage's points in your own words and get a firm understanding of Paul's meaning in the passage.

1 and 2 Corinthians: Paul's letters to the church in Corinth, written about 55 and 56 AD respectively, address specific issues that were plaguing this first century church. Corinth was known for its corrupt wealth and also for its pagan strongholds. And those influences were negatively impacting Corinthian congregations. Let's face it, the Corinthian church was a mess. Paul admonishes them to humble themselves, serve one another rather than lord over each other, stamp out the immorality, and be good examples of Christ-followers to those around them. Paul wrote II Corinthians to this same church about a year later. It's a letter filled with strong emotion, as he sets out to convince the church that suffering is a natural part of his life as a faithful follower of Christ. He defends his lowly state not as a sign of God's judgment, but as a sign that he is following faithfully and joyfully in the footsteps of Christ. This was a haughty church, and Paul deals strongly with them.

Galatians: I particularly love Galatians because the author, Paul, takes a firm and direct approach to some theological issues that came up in the church at Galatia. Writing about 48 AD, his main thesis is the defense of the doctrine of salvation by grace alone, through faith alone. It seems false teachers had come into the church and begun to undermine that doctrine, instead arguing that the new gentile Christians needed to become Jewish first (demonstrated by circumcision) before becoming Christian. "*O foolish Galatians!*" Paul exclaims in his exasperation. "*Who has bewitched you?*" Do you see the potential for a wonderfully rousing reading? Watch for numerous contrasts between faith and works, law and grace, sonship and slavery, and life in the Spirit versus the desires of the flesh.

Ephesians: This letter was delivered to the church at Ephesus by Paul's trusted friend Tychicus (TICH-eh-cuss) to let them know how he was doing while under arrest in Rome, around 62 AD. It contains general teaching, particularly about how Christ has united all creation to himself and all nations to himself and to one another. Again, the central idea is that faith is the avenue by which we come to God, by God-given grace. Ephesians 2:8 is a key verse, "For by grace you have been saved through faith. And this is not your own doing; it is the gift of God, not a result of works, so that no one may boast."

Philippians: Paul wrote this letter to the Christians at Philippi most likely from prison in Rome, also around 62 AD. This letter has a bittersweet, yet encouraging tone, as Paul was fairly certain that he would be put to death in the near future. He commends the spiritual growth he sees in the church and encourages them to continue strong in the faith. Despite telling them to expect suffering as a normal part of serving Christ, he encourages them to remain joyful in the face of it. Paul commends prayer and encourages them to grow together in Christ, in their community of faith.

Colossians: This short letter written by Paul, once again around 62 AD from prison in Rome, is addressed to the church in Colossae. It focuses very much on Christ and his dominion over all things. Paul admonishes the Colossians to, "so walk in him, rooted and built up in him and established in the faith, just as you were taught, abounding in thanksgiving." Paul exhorts the church to reject syncretism and appreciate Christ's sufficiency. Although this book is short, it contains many of Paul's long, complicated, multi-phrased sentences. Take care with these to draw out all the richness.

1 and 2 Thessalonians: The two letters to the church at Thessalonica both center on the second coming of Christ. Apparently there was some confusion and fear surrounding what to expect and when that might happen. The church was also concerned about what would happen to its members who had already died. In addition, they were getting a taste of persecution as followers of Jesus. With so much changing in their world with the coming of Christ, all areas of life were now in a bit of confusion. Paul spends some time in these letters encouraging the church to hold on to their faith and put their trust in Christ.

1 and 2 Timothy: These two personal letters from Paul to his apprentice, Timothy, teach the younger man many practical things about the Christian experience and the important principle that holding to the *true* gospel results in an authentic godly life. The first letter was written in the mid-60s AD, after Paul's first imprisonment in Rome. Paul's second letter to young Timothy was written during his second imprisonment in Rome, where Paul clearly understood that he would soon be facing execution. In response, this second letter is a bold encouragement to Timothy to hold firm to the faith and to persevere in the face of opposition.

Titus: In this short letter from Paul to his missionary colleague, Titus, Paul focuses on the connection between the teaching of the authentic gospel with the living of an authentic life, that belief and behavior are inextricably tied together. Out of this idea flows the practical ways that life will be ordered as a result of right belief. Paul gives guidelines for how men, women, and even bondservants should conduct themselves in a God-honoring way.

Philemon: The Apostle Paul, accompanied by Timothy, wrote this letter to a friend, Philemon (Feye-LEE-mon) and to the church that met in his home, somewhere around 62 AD. This letter explains an amazing situation that occurred in the early church that had far-reaching implications for the larger church. Philemon, a wealthy man of Colossae, had a servant named Onesimus (Oh-NESS-i-muss). This servant apparently stole money from his master and fled to Rome, hoping to blend in and disappear. As providence would have it, Onesimus met Paul, converted to Christianity, and experienced a profound change of life. Paul and Onesimus became dear friends, and it was soon clear to Paul that the trespass and broken relationship between his friends, the servant and the master, would have to be repaired. Paul sends Onesimus back to Philemon with this letter, as an appeal for forgiveness and a reordering of the relationship from servant/master to brother/brother.

Hebrews: The author of Hebrews is unknown, though we can glean from its contents that he knew Timothy, and that he was not an eyewitness of Jesus. Many scholars believe this book was actually a sermon, because it lacks many of the hallmarks of a letter such as a salutation and closing. Its name comes from the fact that it engages exclusively with Hebrew history. The book argues for Jesus as the culmination of and superiority to the prophets, priests, and sacrifices through Israel's history. The author clearly aims to prove that Jesus is who God's chosen people have been waiting for since the beginning. This book contains the extensive litany of Hebrew heroes many have dubbed "the Hall of Faith," introduced by the admonition that "faith is the assurance of things hoped for, the conviction of things not seen."

James: James the Just, as he was called, was the brother of Jesus, who converted to Christianity as an adult, and became the leader of the church in Jerusalem. He wrote this letter to his fellow Jews sometime before 62 AD, when he was executed for his faith. The book begins as a letter but shifts into a strongly worded collection of commands, tinged with satire and practicality. Paired with Paul's teachings on faith, James's strong admonition toward good works gives us a good balance of the two necessary components of the Christian life. "So also faith by itself, if it does not have works, is dead" (*James 2:17*).

1 and 2 Peter: The apostle Peter, close friend of Jesus and witness of most of the gospel events, wrote these two letters probably to gentile churches in Asia Minor. The second letter was written just before his death, around 64–67 AD. Peter focuses on encouraging the Christians to persevere through persecution and to look to Christ for hope, not only for their eternal satisfaction, but for joy in their present earthly lives. Instructing on the dangers of false teaching and how to deal with it in the church, Peter uses an authoritative tone and gives urgent commands for the people to hold fast to their faith.

1, 2, and 3 John: The John named as the author in the actual text is most widely held to be the apostle John who wrote the fourth gospel. They were written toward the end of the first century, around 90 AD. These three short letters each have their own recipients and purposes. 1 John is very likely written to the churches surrounding the area where he lived out the end of his life, which he listed in the Book of Revelation: Smyrna, Pergamum, Thyatira, Sardis, Philadelphia, and Laodicea. This letter lacks a clear outline but emphasizes several themes: true teaching, obedience to Christ in daily life, and fervent devotion for Christ and his church. 2 John is addressed to "the elect lady," which probably refers to a church, rather than an individual, since he later refers to another church as, "your elect sister." Again, as an elder statesman of the church, he offers wonderful wisdom about devout Christian living and insight into finer doctrinal issues. 3 John is a very short letter, just thirteen verses, addressed to a man named Gaius with three basic topics: supporting Christian missionaries, church discipline, and good works as evidence of true faith.

Jude: Jude was another brother of Jesus himself, and the authorship of this short one-chapter book is not in dispute. Jude warns his readers in the strongest language to defend the faith from false teachers who have infiltrated the church: libertines who were enticing believers away from the certain hope of salvation in Jesus Christ. He writes "appealing to you to contend for the faith that was once for all delivered to the saints" (*Jude 3*).

Apocalyptic Literature

Revelation: The Bible contains one book in the apocalyptic genre, the Book of the Revelation to John, commonly referred to simply as "Revelation." Its uniqueness stems from the fact that though the apostle penned the book, its author is Jesus, who gave John the wondrously detailed vision. "Apocalypse" is a Greek-derived word that means "revelation, disclosure, or unveiling," rather than the common usage of the word to mean "end times epic last battle." This book relates the fantastic, detailed, and challenging vision John experienced toward the end of his life, describing end-times events in the spiritual and physical realm. It harkens back to prophecies from Old Testament prophets who were given similar visions: Daniel, Ezekiel, and Zechariah. This vision describes, with illusion and symbolism, the battle between Almighty God and his armies against Satan and his minions. (Spoiler alert: God wins.) As a reader, the goal here is not to be able to figure out every image and event in the passage, but to read it as if you are seeing the vision with your own eyes, as John did.

BIBLIOGRAPHY

The Anglican Church in North America. *The Book of Common Prayer.* Anglican Liturgy Press, 2019.

Bevins, Winfield. *Ever Ancient, Ever New: The Allure of Liturgy for a New Generation.* Grand Rapids: Zondervan, 2019.

Challies, Tim and Josh Byers. *A Visual Theology Guide to the Bible: Seeing and Knowing God's Word.* Grand Rapids: Zondervan, 2019.

Fee, Gordon D. and Douglas Stuart. *Reading the Bible for All Its Worth.* Grand Rapids: Zondervan, Fourth Edition, 2014.

McDowell, Josh and Sean McDowell. *Evidence that Demands a Verdict: Life-Changing Truth for a Skeptical World.* Nashville: Thomas Nelson, 2017.

"State of the Bible 2017: Top Findings." *Barna Group*, April 4, 2017, www.barna.com/research/state-bible-2017-top-findings/

Wilkin, Jen. *Women of the Word: How to Study the Bible with Both Our Hearts and Our Minds.* Wheaton: Crossway, 2014.

ACKNOWLEDGEMENTS

I'm greatly indebted to these friends who read the book in its early stages and helped me stay on track and true to the book's purpose: Ian Andrews, Gary Ester, Ruth Fengler, Christy Fuller, Julie George, Bryan Hunter, Elizabeth Hunter, and John Suan.

Many thanks to the clergy who gave the manuscript a thumbs-up; I would not have wanted to share this with the Church without their input: The Rev. Deacon Carol Brooks, The Rev. Don McLane, The Rev. Theron Walker, The Rev. Deacon Jean Wolfe. I am grateful to my rector, The Rev. Justin Lokey, who prodded me to actually put pen to paper and share my training with my fellow lay readers.

Many thanks also my editor, Katie Chambers, who carefully vetted the manuscript, and to my writing coach, Jed Jurchenko, for all his help and encouragement. Special thanks to my husband Ted, my companion on the Christian journey for over 30 years, and my daughter Emma, who reminds me of the grace of God every day.

FOR FURTHER
LAY READER TRAINING

Contact us through our website www.goodshepherdpublishing.com training to learn how your lay reader team can enjoy a one-day hands-on training with Ms. Telisak at your location. Also find more resources to support your lay reader ministry at www.goodshepherdpublishing.com/eloquentlayreader/resources

Made in the USA
Columbia, SC
12 January 2022

54137846R00070